How to *REALLY* Start Your Own Business

Inc. MAGAZINE PRESENTS

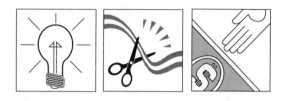

HOW TO *REALLY* START YOUR OWN BUSINESS

* *

A Step-by-Step Guide Featuring
Insights and Advice from the Founders of

Crate & Barrel ▪ David's Cookies
Celestial Seasonings ▪ Pizza Hut
Silicon Technology ▪ Esprit Miami

BY DAVID E. GUMPERT

How To Really Start Your Own Business

First Edition

Designers: Susan Dahl, Susan RZ Slovinsky

This publication is designed to provide accurate and authoritative information in regard to the subject matter covered. It is sold with the understanding that the publisher is not engaged in rendering legal, accounting, or other professional service. If legal advice or other expert assistance is required, the services of a competent professional should be sought.

Library of Congress Catalog Number: 91–72604

ISBN: 0–9626146–2–9

•

For my parents
Leonore and Louis Gumpert

TABLE OF CONTENTS

PREFACE

This book has been four years in the making.

It began as a project to produce a video, "How to *Really* Start Your Own Business," that would be informative, entertaining, and realistic — that would go well beyond the predictable material on starting a business. The team from *Inc.* and Karl Lorimar Video (now Warner Home Video) that produced the two-hour videotape that resulted — of which I was fortunate enough to be a part — truly agonized over its organization and presentation.

One of the challenges of putting that video together was selecting from the incredible amount of useful footage we shot with nine successful entrepreneurs. The video, which was originally going to be one hour, was extended to ninety minutes. When that proved insufficient, it expanded to two hours.

Even two hours turned out to be limiting. The videotape, however, was a huge success. It won the American Video Award for Best Business Program (1987) — the video industry's equivalent of an Oscar. It scored extremely high marks in feedback surveys from the thousands of individuals who purchased it.

But those of us involved in producing the tape knew we had not completed our effort. We couldn't escape the fact that so much interesting and important material had gone unused.

By 1990 we had determined to solve that problem; I would write a book that would build on the original tape. It would be organized in the same way as the tape and would contain many of its themes, but it would do much more. It would dig deeper and incorporate many insights and lessons that couldn't be included in the tape due to time constraints. It would also provide extensive worksheets and lessons so readers could evaluate their own business ideas and plans in a realistic way. The hope was that we would provide the depth and detail that only a book format is capable of.

The experts in small business who reviewed this book prior to publication feel we accomplished our goal — and then some. You the reader will be the ultimate judge.

ACKNOWLEDGMENTS

While the author gets much of the credit for writing a book, there are invariably many people working to assure it gets completed and is of high quality. That was especially so with this book.

I'd like to thank those people here. The order in which I name them is not necessarily reflective of their contributions, since I don't think I can prioritize their efforts.

I can say from personal experience working with publishers that the publishing group at *Inc.* has quickly learned how to make an author feel comfortable and wanted. Jan Spiro, Mary Ellen Mullaney, Bob LaPointe, and Joel Novak have all been extremely supportive of this project, and I can't thank them enough. And Candace Harris has worked behind the scenes from the start of the video project to make critical events occur.

Thanks also go to Harold Klein of Teletime Video Productions. He conducted the interviews for the video that served as the basis for much that is contained in this book. He also shared his technological expertise to enable me to review the interviews in the most convenient formats possible.

Sue Dahl's creative design efforts and flexible production approach made the writing process more productive and time-effective than I could have hoped. Jeanne Zimmermann's thoughtful editing made the writing much smoother than it might otherwise have been. Susan Slovinsky came through with another dynamite cover.

When I needed transcribing help, and related editorial assistance, three people responded in a very timely and professional way—my mother, Leonore Gumpert, Jan Flynn, and Candace Wright.

And when I needed the help of experts to review my writing, I was also extremely fortunate. Joseph Iandiorio, a Waltham, Massachusetts, attorney who specializes in intellectual property, saved me some embarrassing errors in my discussion of how to protect entrepreneurs' ideas. Bernard Tenenbaum of Fairleigh Dickinson University, Bill Bygrave of Babson College, and Jerry Arnold of the University of Southern California also provided important suggestions that helped me give the book greater depth.

I also must acknowledge the expertise I gained from being a part of the Technology Executive Roundtable, an educational and networking organization for entrepreneurs sponsored nationally by Digital Equipment Corp. I learned much about intellectual property, managing people, and market research from its informative meetings. Thanks to Joan Jacobs and Robert Weisman.

Of course, this book could never have happened had it not been for the generous input received from nine very special entrepreneurs: Mo Siegel, founder of Celestial Seasonings; David Liederman, founder of David's Cookies; Frank Carney, founder of Pizza Hut; Gordon Segal, founder of Crate & Barrel; George Kachajian, founder of Silicon Technology; Christine Martindale, founder of Esprit Miami; James Lowry, founder of James Lowry Associates; Betsy Tabak, founder of Tabak and Associates; and Jim Buck, founder of Northern Timber Framing.

Finally, I need to thank my family—Jean, Jason, and Laura—who put up with the clearly crazy schedule that was necessary to get this book completed.

How to *REALLY* Start Your Own Business

REALITY THERAPY FOR ENTREPRENEURS

As you peruse this book, you may ask yourself, Why do we need another book about starting a business?

That is a natural question, since many books have been written about the topic. The answer is really the guiding philosophy behind this book and what I believe makes it unique. It also helps explain the title, *How to* Really *Start Your Own Business.*

Even though many books have been written about starting a business, this is the first that provides a truly realistic view of the process — reality therapy, as it were, for would-be entrepreneurs. Many other books tend to fall into either of two traps: In an effort to be positive and enthusiastic, they make the start-up process sound easier than it is, or they are so academic they make the start-up process appear mundane and technical.

In my view, starting a business is a major life event. As such, it is neither easy nor boring. It is a huge challenge that is frequently misunderstood by would-be entrepreneurs.

Starting a business is tough enough under the best of circumstances. To go into it with a misguided view of the special demands and requirements is to invite disaster. The reality therapy offered in this book comes from two sources: a handful of highly successful entrepreneurs who have recalled in detail their start-up experiences and my many years of observing and reporting on start-up entrepreneurs.

Reality therapy is essential for today's start-up entrepreneur. By knowing what hurdles lie ahead, you can anticipate and plan more accurately and thus save yourself unpleasant surprises. I even feel that if you read this book and decide against starting a particular business because you determine it is too risky or you aren't cut out for being an entrepreneur, then you have been well served. Not all great-sounding ideas are truly viable, and not everyone is cut out to be an entrepreneur. Starting a business that fails, while not the end of the world, is expensive and emotionally upsetting.

■ Getting Married

In line with my comment describing the start-up process as a major life event, the life event it most closely compares with is marriage. That's primarily because, like marriage, it's much easier to get started in your own business than it is to make it work over the long haul. (The marriage comparison reappears later in the book, in considering relationships with partners.) Hundreds of thousands of people start businesses each year. But from 60% to 80% (no one knows for certain) get "divorced" from their businesses within five years.

There's no magical solution to such a problem, but the best one available isn't unlike that required to make a marriage work: Know what you're getting into and what's necessary to make it succeed.

How to Really *Start Your Own Business* is intended to help you begin a company the right way — allowing you to steer around the more difficult hurdles being thrown into the paths of all new businesses.

■ The Deception

One of the confounding factors in the start-up process today is that in many respects, starting a business has never been easier. A number of important trends helped lead to the boom in entrepreneurship in the 1980s and seem likely to play an even larger role during the fast-changing 1990s.

But in important ways, these trends are deceiving. They make it easier to open a business, but they make it difficult to lay a proper foundation for growth and long-term success. These trends include the following:

- *Increasingly sophisticated technology at ever-lower costs.* Personal computers, fax machines, portable phones, voice mail, and other equipment have become fixtures of the modern office. For start-up entrepreneurs, though, they play an added role. Such tools enable them to do two things that entrepreneurs of a previous generation could never hope to accomplish:

    1. Get started with fewer people. A personal computer may obviate the need for a secretary and a bookkeeper at the start. Voice mail eliminates the need for a receptionist. A portable phone enables the start-up entrepreneur to be available for calls from prospective customers — while driving to meet with other prospects. Such improved productivity allows the new entrepreneur to save huge sums in start-up costs. The technology may be acquired for less than $10,000 — even $5,000 if one knows his or her way around and bargain-hunts. If you figure the cost of each new hire from $30,000 to $60,000 annually (including Social Security taxes and benefits), it becomes apparent that being able to eliminate the need for two, three, or more people adds up pretty quickly.

    2. Look well established. All that sophisticated technology also makes even the smallest business look very professional — and established. It's possible for the start-up entrepreneur to create professional-looking stationery, presentations, and proposals from day one. Voice mail and a fax machine similarly convey an impression of stability and experience.

Moreover, the cost/benefit ratios of technology promise to become more favorable to entrepreneurs. Today's computers are faster, have more memory, and cost less than those of five years ago. The same goes for portable phones and fax machines. And you can bet that the trend will continue.

• **Subcontracting by major corporations.** As major corporations have restructured and reorganized, they have in many cases moved to reduce their overhead by doing fewer tasks in-house. They are subcontracting many jobs they used to do themselves, ranging from doing public relations to producing the instruction booklets that accompany their products to maintaining their grounds. Increasingly, the beneficiaries of this trend are small businesses.

The start-up landscaper who can line up a contract handling a major corporation's nearby sales office may be off to a great beginning. In some cases, an employee leaving a corporation to start a company may be able to do his or her job on a consulting basis, enabling the individual to have clients immediately.

• **Accessible marketing data.** Not long ago, someone thinking about starting a business had to do a lot of legwork to track down marketing information. Some was contained in books that were already out of date when printed. Some was in magazines stored in the depths of the local library, where one could spend days seeking the essential data. Now, thanks to electronic data bases, it's much easier and cheaper for entrepreneurs to obtain industry studies, competitor information, and related data. And it will become even easier as new storage mechanisms like CD-ROM become more widely available. These will enable entrepreneurs to search through vast quantities of reference material as well as lists of prospective buyers to determine far more accurately the existence of a viable market.

• *Acceptance of low-overhead operations.* It used to be that start-up entrepreneurs went to great extremes to give the appearance of stability and experience. They would rent high-priced office space, acquire fancy furniture, and lease expensive cars to impress potential customers. Today's discerning customers are often turned off by opulent trappings — whether by start-up or established businesses. They know who winds up paying the costs associated with high overhead. That changing perception helps make it easier for the start-up entrepreneur to begin his or her business from the home or an out-of-the-way suburban or rural location — and attract growing legions of value-oriented customers.

■ The Land Mines to Avoid

It's only after the business has started that entrepreneurs often learn about the new — and dangerous — age of business ownership. A fast-changing environment, which favors entrepreneurs in the earliest stages, can conspire against them once they are up and running. Consider the following:

• *More intense competition than ever.* The growing availability of information and the speed with which it travels can become a liability once you have achieved some success. As soon as you begin to do well, other entrepreneurs will hear about it and begin to compete with you. Think back to how quickly competing video-rental stores, fast-food outlets, and quick-print establishments opened in your town once the first outlets began doing well.

The competition doesn't just come from other entrepreneurs. Increasingly, major corporations — both domestic and foreign — are honing in on markets that they might have considered too small a few years back. They are opening chains of restaurants, dry-cleaning establishments, consulting firms, and many other kinds of businesses. Because corporations often have tremendous financial resources to put behind advertising, these competitors can make life quite difficult for the early-stage entrepreneur.

• *Fast-changing customer demands and tastes.* As people become better informed, they become more demanding buyers. They want the best values, the latest features, the most attractive prices — and if they don't get these from you, they will go elsewhere.

   The problem for the start-up entrepreneur is that what consumers prefer keeps changing. Restaurant owners suddenly discovered that more people wanted to take home prepared food and save money. Video-store operators found that numbers of people wanted their videos delivered. If you don't find out about such changes before your customers get the new product or service from somewhere else, you are in big trouble.

• *Need to be global.* You've no doubt heard about the movement toward a so-called global economy. What that means for the start-up entrepreneur is that it is difficult to base your business entirely on local customers and local economic conditions. Many start-up entrepreneurs learned this lesson the hard way in Texas during the mid and late 1980s and in New England during the early 1990s. In many cases, the businesses that survived and prospered in the face of regional recessions were those that did business nationally and internationally.

• *Raising growth capital more difficult.* Lenders and investors of all types are increasingly skittish about committing to start-up and early-stage businesses. The reasons are varied, but should your start-up business suddenly prosper and grow to the point that you need to raise money, you may encounter difficulties obtaining that money from traditional sources. As I discuss in Chapter 7, some less traditional sources are filling part of the gap. But a rapidly growing business that is unable to find capital can encounter serious long-term difficulties coming up with essential cash.

• **Harder to find and keep the best people.** Demographic forces are at work that are reducing the skilled labor pool during the 1990s. The implication is that small businesses are increasingly in competition with large corporations for workers. Corporations can typically afford to pay higher salaries and offer better benefit programs than smaller companies. So more and more small businesses are scrambling to get and retain good workers.

■ The Real Challenge

If you're starting a business, it is essential that you do it right. That means carefully evaluating your idea, getting the best people to work with you, anticipating your cash flow, writing an effective business plan, and accomplishing the endless additional tasks that are part and parcel of the start-up process.

As I pointed out, it's possible to get up and running doing much less than what this book advises. What's important in today's environment, however, is to build a foundation for long-term success. That's what this book is intended to help you accomplish.

CHAPTER ONE

THE IDEA

*"I went into a cookie store in Berkeley,
California, and it was like finding religion."*

∙∙∙∙∙∙∙∙∙∙∙∙∙∙∙∙∙∙∙∙∙∙∙∙∙∙∙∙∙

David Liederman, founder of David's Cookies

If you ask three well-known entrepreneurs how they came up with the ideas for their businesses, you'll get three reasonably simple answers.

- *The idea for starting **Pizza Hut** came to Frank Carney from the landlady of a building next to the Kansas City grocery store where he worked during the mid-1950s. "There was a little bar next door, and the people who owned the building wanted the bar moved out. It wasn't a good neighborhood for a bar. So the landlady came over and talked to my brother and suggested that he start a pizza place. We did not have the idea, and we also didn't have any money. So we borrowed $300 from my mother. Neither one of us even knew how to make pizza. I had only eaten pizza once before we started and my brother had eaten it while he was in the service."*

- *Mo Siegel started **Celestial Seasonings** in the early 1970s based in large measure on a trip. "I went to Europe and I read about the success of tea in Europe," he recalls. "So there was a track record in Europe that herb tea worked. If there hadn't been a track record somewhere in the*

11

world that the idea was acceptable to a lot of people, I don't know that I would have done it. . . . Not only was the European market very good, but the health wave in America was starting up, and no one had filled that niche of providing a caffeine-free product."

• *The idea for* **Crate & Barrel,** *the national chain of home-furnishing stores, came to Gordon Segal during the early 1960s when he was living in Chicago as a young newlywed. "We had just gotten married a year prior, and we were looking for good design. We had good taste and no money, and we said there must be some place where you can buy tasteful [home furnishings] at not a whole lot of money. There were beautiful stores in Chicago that had very expensive products. And then there were inexpensive places that had ugly product. But there was no place where you could find beautiful product at an inexpensive price. . . . Then we delved into how to do it."*

So on the surface, Frank Carney got his start-up idea from a landlady, Mo Siegel got his inspiration from traveling in Europe, and Gordon Segal got his idea because of his own difficulty finding tasteful, inexpensive home furnishings. It seems so simple and straightforward that you want to grab an idea and rush out to imitate these fabulously successful entrepreneurs.

The truth is, though, that if you're at the point of thinking seriously about starting your own business, you've probably had more than one idea for a business. The situation you're more likely facing isn't how to come up with an idea but how to come up with *the* idea.

There's a tendency to think that the right idea for a business comes from some profound — even mystical — inspiration. There's also a tendency — reinforced by many books that have been written about starting and running a business — to believe that the inspiration comes from an academic-type search or from sophisticated brain-storming. According to this theory, if you talk with enough entrepreneurs, accountants and business brokers; go to enough trade shows and libraries; and read enough issues of

Commerce Business Daily and *Electronic Business*, you'll stimulate
that be-all and end-all of ideas.

But if you examine closely the three entrepreneurs just quoted,
you don't find many splashes of such inspiration. Instead, you find
a deceptively complex process at work.

■ Beyond the Obvious

The ideas for Pizza Hut, Celestial Seasonings, Crate & Barrel,
and other successful companies seem simple on the surface. But
there is much more to them than is apparent at first glance. These
other components become clearer when the entrepreneurs are
questioned in detail about how their businesses started. These
factors are extremely important to anyone considering starting a
business and include the following:

• *Personal goals.* Successful entrepreneurs will invariably tell you
that starting and building their own business represents the
fulfillment of a long-standing personal goal. Here is how Mo
Siegel puts it: "From a very early age, I realized that I would
probably be a very lousy employee. Owning your own business
is a mixture of sweet and sour, hot and cold, love and hate, fun
and hell."

James Lowry, founder of James A. Lowry Associates, a
Chicago-based consulting firm, is even more explicit: "I think
anyone wanting to start a business... should put on a piece of
paper not a business plan but a personal plan. The business plan
will come later. A personal plan is something where I say, 'Here
is where I want to be ten years from now. I want to have a net
worth of X millions of dollars. I want to have an annual income of
X number of dollars. I want to employ anywhere from three to
fifty people. I want to be able to travel; I don't want to be able to
travel. But something that is very germane to that individual,
that's very important to that individual, because business is so

tough and it's so demanding that unless you are doing something you want to do with the people you want to do it with and the style you want to do it in with the kind of return on your investment that you aspire to, you won't be happy and you won't be a good business-person."

Did Lowry take his own advice? "Yes, I did. I did it when I was on assignment with this other firm. I was in Tanzania, of all places, and one day I took out two days in my life, I sat down and drew up objectives. I drew up objectives for health, I did objectives of where I wanted to be at age 50. What kind of shape do I want to be in? Do I want to be able to run a mile, two miles, swim a mile? I set those objectives down, and that was when I was twenty-eight. I also set down objectives about what kind of income I wanted, what kind of lifestyle, how much travel. It was surprising because I wrote it all out and I kept it. And ten years later I picked it up and I read it, and I had surpassed every goal that I had established for myself."

In other words, the idea must be accompanied by a personal desire to start and operate a business. It must be part of what you want out of life, just as getting married, having children, buying a house, and pursuing certain hobbies are reflections of your personal desires. If starting and running a business don't fit into your personal goals, then the ideas you come up with have little significance because they stand little chance of being converted into successful businesses.

- **Prior work experience.** If there is one factor that stands out as being a key part of any idea, it is previous work experience. While it is not an absolute prerequisite, prior experience seems to be part and parcel of the idea more often than it is not.

  Take the case of Frank Carney. When you ask him about the idea, he talks about the landlady who suggested a pizza shop as a way to get rid of an inappropriate bar. But the reality is that Carney had many years of experience in the food industry before starting Pizza Hut. Here is how he describes the situation:

"My dad, whom I didn't know very well — he died of a heart attack when I was in the fourth grade — left his job and went to work with a partner and started a grocery store, Carney's Supermarket [in Wichita]. And when he died of a heart attack, there were seven of us with my mother, and the family ran the store. So we kind of grew up on the other side of the food business. . . . My mother remarried a man with four children, and there were a dozen of us living out of the grocery store, so we weren't exactly flush with money. It was not tough but tight."

When asked what assets he had when starting up, Carney states: "The main asset that my brother and I had was that we really knew all the functions of a small business because of our experience with the grocery store — rotating product, handling money, ordering, and all the various things you do to run a small business. . . . I think the lesson here is that people. . . get some experience in the business they're thinking of starting. . . . If a person wants to start a restaurant and has never been in the business before, he'd better work for somebody. Otherwise, he may do some dumb things that he could have avoided. The best thing is to work in a restaurant to see how the restaurant business works and then, after contact with consumers and learning the back end of the operation, decide whether this is the kind of business to start."

- *Knowledge base.* Call it information, intelligence, or familiarity. The underlying message is that entrepreneurs must have as much knowledge as possible to support any idea for a new business. David Liederman, founder of David's Cookies, a chain of chocolate-chip cookie stores, explains the notion best:

  "To have a chance of success, it is by far most important to have an idea, a concept, that you know more about than anyone else. I am not a doctor, so I couldn't open a bypass-surgery clinic. I am constantly amazed when entrepreneurs say they want to do this kind of cake or brownie, and they don't know how to bake or how to put it into production or about purchasing or distribution. You have to know what you want to sell."

The other side of the coin, says Mo Siegel, is operating on instinct or hunches. "There is no substitute for a lot of knowledge. You can work on gut instincts, but gut instincts can get you into trouble. I have had a lot of times where I have had gut instincts and I was dead wrong. I was convinced it was right, but it took a little more knowledge for me to understand that I was really going in the wrong direction. . . .When I started Celestial Seasonings, I did not have a college education. Without a master's degree out of Harvard or Stanford, there were a lot of things that I had no idea about in business. For years I rode my bicycle to work listening to Peter Drucker on cassette tapes and to all kinds of other management information on cassettes. I read like crazy. . . .You have to put in the time to get the knowledge base or else you don't have anything to work with."

Certainly, the knowledge base is acquired most naturally by having the appropriate work or business experience. As Siegel suggests, it can also be acquired by asking questions, listening, reading, and doing research.

- **Solving a problem.** Entrepreneurial lore is filled with stories of individuals whose business idea was born when they couldn't find a particular food or type of clothing or encountered a safety problem. A classic case involves George Kachajian, founder of Silicon Technology Corp. of Oakland, New Jersey, a maker of equipment that slices silicon for semiconductor chips used in computers, televisions, and other electronic equipment.

  He describes graphically how he was a corporate engineer visiting a plant in Michigan. "I walked into the [silicon] slicing room, and I saw one of the operators cut his hand on the blade, and the blood came on my shirt. I caught the guy falling away from the machine and gave him some quick first aid and got some help, and the whole event was traumatic. I thought there had to be a better way than the method that was being used at that time. So I took my first hard look at a slicing machine at that moment and realized that the blade was exposed and the operator's safety risk was high. It was a trauma that stayed with me a couple of weeks, and I could not get it out of my head. Finally, I decided that a simple way of eliminating the hazard would be to rotate the entire operation from a vertical to a horizontal blade... and cover the bottom half of the blade with a piece of sheet metal so the operator couldn't possibly cut himself unless he forced his finger up into the exposed area of the blade. . . . I realized this was the opportunity I had been looking for for many years."

Similarly, Gordon Segal's difficulty trying to find reasonably priced and tasteful home decorations stimulated the idea for Crate & Barrel. He even feels that his lack of experience in home furnishings helped him: "I think that one of our great benefits is that we didn't work for anyone else, we didn't know anything about retail [home furnishings], and we had never done anything according to how it was supposed to be done."

Yet for Kachajian and even for Segal, it would be a mistake to think that simply seeing a problem and devising a solution were all that was necessary to come up with the idea. Kachajian was able to spot the problem with machinery and come up with an idea for an improved tool based on his eighteen years of experience as an engineer for a major corporation.

Segal had important business experience as well, which he credits with helping him formulate his initial business idea: "I had grown up with a family that was in the restaurant business. The restaurant business is the ultimate retail business, and I think the understanding of how to serve a customer and how to make him happy and how to have a sense of urgency I got literally from the restaurant business."

He continues: "I worked from an early age in my father's restaurant. I spent five or six years serving customers and making them happy and achieving a sense of urgency and a sense of service, and I knew I liked that. I knew there was a joy I got out of making people happy in a face-to-face relationship, and that is what you have to have — that joy you get from a good retail sale or a good restaurant customer served properly is unique. You can't get it from any other business."

- **Serving a niche.** A market niche is a specialized and easily identifiable group of potential customers that a company targets. By its nature, a market niche is a subset of something much larger. For instance, a chain of diet clinics intended for baby boomers may conclude that it can't effectively go after all the 77-million-plus people in that category, and it may instead concentrate on a niche, such as female baby boomers with annual incomes between $30,000 and $50,000 who have at least one child.

  The idea stage might seem a bit early to be discussing a niche. But in talking with entrepreneurs about how they came up with their ideas, it becomes clear that the market niche is an important part of the original idea for many entrepreneurs.

  James Lowry had spent eight years working with one of America's largest management consulting firms when he came up with the idea for his own consulting firm in Chicago: "I saw a market niche. You hear a lot about what is a market niche. In this particular case, there were a lot of consulting firms in Chicago but very few consulting on minority issues. At times, I was kind of sensitive to the fact that I was put in this minority niche, but after a few years of going to the bank, I didn't feel bad."

  How did Lowry actually determine his niche? "There were a lot of chief executives and vice presidents of human resources saying that they would love to hire more minorities if they could just find them. I guess when I started looking at the marketplace and I surveyed the whole nation, I found a lot of consulting firms. . . . But there was not in America at that time [1975] what I would call a full-service minority consulting firm — a firm that could offer a whole range of consulting services to a CEO of a major corporation."

Lowry's approach wasn't unlike that of Mo Siegel's in coming up with the idea for Celestial Seasonings. Certainly there was no way a new company could appeal to everyone with a product that was nearly unknown in the United States in the early 1970s — herbal tea. As he says, "Celestial Seasonings was an idea of providing very high quality herb tea that could be used hot or iced. In the beginning we filled a niche that was a hot soothing beverage at night that had no caffeine but lots of flavor. We were a flavor opportunity, a soothing opportunity, a noncaffeine opportunity."

- **The right attitude.** Many ideas for new businesses stem from a desire to get rich quickly. Some magazines, franchises, and consultants play into that desire in an effort to promote their products or services. According to successful entrepreneurs, however, starting a business with this approach is definitely the wrong attitude to have.

  Not that money shouldn't be an important part of the equation. But the money, when it comes, will likely come only much later than many of us would like, and after considerable effort. Says Mo Siegel: "Working for yourself is not all that easy. You often have years of a labor of love where you don't make any money, the hours are incredibly long. I think it is important to figure what the reward is going to be for it. . . . If you give your best and you are doing something that people need... you are going to get rewarded all the way along, even if you aren't making a lot of money in the beginning."

  Gordon Segal expresses a similar attitude: "It has to be an inner vision. It can't be, well, if we build this we can make so much money. It can't be just singularly profit motivated. I think profit has to be very important. You have to run it like a professional business, especially as you grow, but I definitely think there has to be a philosophy and a vision that you have, and certainly as you grow the business, you could enthuse other people with it."

- **Total commitment.** Part of the reason the idea is really a small part of the business start-up equation is that putting it into effect is usually so difficult. Successful entrepreneurs know just how difficult it is, and they stress that individuals trying to formulate an idea also try to factor in that they must be totally committed to success.

  Frank Carney puts it this way: "You have to have drive and you have to have that entrepreneurial spirit that says, 'Damn the torpedoes, full speed ahead!' You have got to have that. You need to balance that with some kind of a honing device, honing in on the customers or honing in on how to make a profit. . . . You have to have directions and goals and that balance of when to make changes, what to listen to."

  Gordon Segal feels that the idea must be analyzed with an eye toward both your own disposition and your role in the market-place. "I think you can only go into business if you have a unique idea, vision, or an ability to execute something much better than anyone you could see on the horizon. I also think it can be the same product that is out there, executed better. I often say that we could run a hardware store better and in a more intelligent fashion than most hardware stores, and we could make it such an exciting hardware store, in execution, that people would walk to the hardware store. . . .You have to be damn sure before you start a business that you have an ability, by execution or by taste or by some interpretation of what you do, to do not an average job but a superior job. I think that what you see today are so many retail stores that are just ho-hum and mediocre and are not delivering anything special and they are in deep financial trouble."

  He concludes: "It really takes an idea, a vision, a concept that you want to achieve. It may be way out there and you have to walk over many valleys, cross many rivers, fall down over many hard rocks, but eventually, if you have the vision, you will get there."

Ultimately, the individual starting a business must have the personal fortitude to develop an idea that is truly superior to what is in existence and then develop it for all it is worth.

■ Asking the Right Questions

Having heard observations from successful entrepreneurs, what do you, the start-up entrepreneur, do to make sure you are on the right track? When entrepreneurs ask me about the potential of an idea for a new business, I invariably ask some probing questions. I am trying to determine the following:

- *Can you clearly articulate the idea?* Ideally, you should be able to describe your idea in a few sentences — fifty words or less. Would-be entrepreneurs often get bogged down when asked to summarize an idea. It's too complicated to explain briefly, they maintain. In my experience, the inability to boil an idea down to a few sentences is a warning sign — evidence that the idea hasn't been clearly thought through.

    Mo Siegel expresses a similar view: "Ideas have got to be very simple. People don't understand complex things. Generally, an idea that is good can be said in two or three sentences. It doesn't require a whole long-winded multipage document to explain an area. There is either an idea or there is not."

- *Where did the idea come from?* A physician I know approached me a few years ago with an idea to subcontract a delivery service to retailers to speed pizza, sandwiches, video rentals, and other items to consumers' homes. The retailers wouldn't have to invest in expensive cars or vans or hire drivers and could still offer a valuable service. Given the fast-changing demands of a competitive marketplace, this was no doubt a very good idea. But given that the individual who came up with the idea was a physician, the idea was probably no more than that — a good idea. He just didn't know enough about either retailers' needs or the intricacies of the consumer business to be able to start such a business. Certainly with enough research it might have been possible to determine whether the idea made sense, but given the demands on his time as a physician, the chances of him being able to carry out that research were slim.

If the owner of a pizza store or even a college student came to me with that idea, I would have been much more optimistic about its chances for success. The pizza-store owner would likely know other store owners and could assess their willingness to contract for such a service and at what price. The college student would know how his or her fellow students might feel about such a service and would be in a position to research it further and perhaps try it out inexpensively.

On the other hand, if the physician had come to me with an idea for a new kind of outpatient health-care facility or therapy treatment for an illness, I might have been more optimistic of his chances for success. Then he would likely have been able to answer basic questions about the feelings of prospective patients, start-up costs, and similar issues.

- **Do you really know the industry?** This question is related to the previous one, except it goes a step further. To return to the example of the physician, I said I might have been more optimistic about his chances for starting a facility or therapy treatment, but even then I would have wanted to know how much he knew about the business of running a medical facility or selling a treatment. It's one thing to work in a health-care facility and quite another to start and operate one. Medical-treatment facilities have their own economics based on occupancy and/or usage rates, relations with insurance providers, overhead, and a host of other factors.

  Most new businesses require an intimate knowledge of the

industry in which you will be starting. Otherwise, you spend too much time reinventing the wheel about such topics as pricing, distribution, overhead costs, and similar matters. Each industry has established norms that can guide the newcomer. Knowing the industry, of course, doesn't mean you have to do things the way they have always been done in that industry. But knowing the industry enables you to make intelligent decisions about what you might do differently so as to create a competitive advantage for your new business. For Mo Siegel, that something different was selling a noncaffeinated tea in an industry that knew only caffeinated ones.

If you don't know the industry from personal or professional experience, you have to go and get it, Siegel suggests. "There is information on any kind of business you want to go into. For example, if you are going into the clothing-store business, there are trade shows that deal specifically with that industry, there are magazines that deal with that industry, there is abundant information. Getting into a trade association is smart. Celestial Seasonings has been in a number of trade associations — one for the supermarkets, one for the gourmet stores. We go to some of the restaurant shows, we go where part of the natural-foods movement assembles. You can sit in on the retail seminars and learn a lot about how to conduct your business properly. When I started Celestial Seasonings, one of the ways I got the knowledge base I needed was that I picked people's brains. I asked the suppliers long series of questions constantly. If you ask a lot of questions and do a lot of listening, you are going to learn in time, and fast."

- **_Have you seen the idea used elsewhere?_** Generally speaking, ideas based on existing businesses are more realistic than those that are unique. David Liederman points out that prior to starting David's Cookies, he launched a business known as Sauciert, which produced gourmet-sauce bases for consumers.

    "You can go into business like Sauciert, a novel business. We had absolutely no competition. It was a unique product. That was the good news. The bad news was overcoming the educational process of saying to Mr. and Mrs. Consumer, 'This is a wonderful sauce base,' and explaining what a sauce base is. It was much more costly than I had anticipated. While I was running around the country doing publicity for Sauciert and going broke, I ran into a cookie store in Berkeley, California, and it was like finding religion. Here was something I could market that people would understand. There was lots of competition, but at least I didn't have to explain to the consumer what a cookie was."

As Gordon Segal put it, the best ideas often involve taking an existing business and doing it better — in his case, unusual home furnishings at affordable prices. There's an old saying among experienced entrepreneurs that seemingly good ideas that have never been implemented have probably not been implemented for a reason.

That is not to say that ideas for unique products and services can't be started quite successfully. Products as important as the light bulb, telephone, television, and automobile, among many others, wouldn't be around if we were completely skeptical of new products. From the viewpoint of the start-up entrepreneur, though, the new and unique product is invariably a much tougher item to sell to investors and customers.

- *What will you do better?* Assuming that your idea is based on a type of business that already exists, a key part of your idea should be particulars about what you will do better than the companies already out there. Too many ideas have more to do with fulfilling some long-held dream to have a business exactly like other businesses. Because the businesses that people have the most contact with are retail ones, the ideas are usually in the retail area. I don't want to appear sexist, but in the case of women, the idea often has to do with opening some kind of boutique — for selling women's clothing, children's books, or upscale imported items.

Men more commonly consider hardware stores, building-supply stores, and restaurants.

Rarely have the would-be entrepreneurs considered just how their business will differ from the many others in existence. A key part of Gordon Segal's idea was that Crate & Barrel would offer high-quality imported home furnishings at reasonable prices, which other Chicago stores weren't doing.

Nor have would-be entrepreneurs usually taken into account that retailing has become even tougher than in the past, as people increasingly shop by catalog or even electronic mail.

- **Has your idea passed the "time test"?** A would-be entrepreneur is typically most excited about an idea at the time he or she actually thinks it up. Whether it's an idea for a new boutique, pet food, or day-care center, it seems so promising, so infallible, so brilliant.

  But how does that same idea look a week, a month, or even six months later? Having thought more about implementation of the idea, the start-up costs, and the kinds of profits it might yield, does it still seem so exciting? Or has some new, totally different idea replaced it?

  If the original idea, perhaps with some modifications, still seems attractive some weeks or months later, then there may be something to it. But if you begin to see significant problems, such as a saturated market or higher-than-expected start-up costs, and the idea begins to pale and excite you less, then you should question whether it's the right one.

- **Are you ready to commit yourself totally to the idea for the next five years or more?** A middle-aged social worker came to me with an idea for starting a manicure business. She felt burned out as a social worker and decided, based on having weekly manicures at a local shop, that this was the business for her. But she had gone a step further than the physician described earlier. She had actually enrolled in a course on manicuring that is required for getting the state license necessary to work on customers.

However, after completing the course, she was beginning to have some doubts. While she was from an upper-middle-class background, the people in the class were mostly lower middle class. She wasn't sure that if her friends came to her for manicures, she would feel comfortable charging them. And though the initial investment for opening a store was within her means, she wasn't convinced she could make that kind of commitment.

The reality was that when push came to shove, she wasn't sure she was prepared to immerse herself fully in the manicure business. She felt very bad, having focused on this idea for more than a year. But from my perspective, her doubts were understandable and, more important, better expressed before opening the business than afterward. There is nothing worse than beginning a business and then discovering that it's not really for you. In that situation, not only are you unhappy, but your chances of failure also increase proportionately. If you are unexcited about your business, that will come through in the way you run it, and you won't do the job customers inevitably demand.

- **Is your idea for a product or a business?** David Liederman says that more often than not, the ideas people have are for the former rather than the latter. "There is an enormous difference between having a product and having a business. Many, many people have a product. People come in the door all the time with great products. A woman came in the other day with a fantastic little fruit-filled cookie, but she told me she could only make two dozen a day. That is not a business."

  One might argue that Mo Siegel's idea for an herbal tea to be known as Red Zinger was really a product. But early on, he had in mind that he would be able to mass-produce it and add other tea flavors. Those factors — being able to produce a product in quantity and add other variations to form a product line — are key to distinguishing between a product and a business.

- **Is this an idea for you or someone else?** This question ties into knowing your capabilities and desires. You may have an idea for a great business and have answered the previous questions satisfactorily, but it could be that you aren't the right person to pull it off. Often, the situation is that the person with the idea doesn't have the organizational or marketing skills to carry it through. That doesn't mean the idea should be abandoned. Perhaps the person with the idea should try to involve others who have the necessary skills. (For more on the people issue, see Chapter 4.)

  It could also be that as good as the idea is, it doesn't fit in with your long-term career or professional goals. If the idea involves a product, you may want to think of approaches for selling it, such as through a licensing agreement or a strategic alliance with a large company. (This is partly a financing issue, addressed more fully in Chapter 7.)

  The point is that you should evaluate the idea in light of your own needs and wants. To succeed, you must take the difficult step of looking at yourself objectively — assessing your strengths and weaknesses as well as your personal goals and objectives.

- **What is the reward potential?** You'll notice that this question is listed last, and for good reason. It almost goes without saying that a principal goal of any business is to make as much money as possible for its owners. However, money shouldn't be the primary motivation behind the idea in the sense of being a get-rich-quick scheme. The entrepreneurs quoted earlier made that point quite emphatically.

  The question is raised here for its guidance value. In some cases, entrepreneurs have an overly optimistic sense of the riches their ideas will lead to. But in other cases, entrepreneurs are pursuing an idea more for love than for money, without realizing that the idea must be completely recast to make it profitable enough to be realistic as a long-term business.

  At this idea stage, you don't need to prepare a detailed cash flow and profit statement. But you should be able to write down some rough estimates of potential start-up costs and investments to determine whether the revenues for a profitable business are really there.

■ The Franchise Factor

In assessing ideas, you should at least think about the possibility of using someone else's idea in the form of a franchise. A franchise is essentially a license to use someone else's name and method of operation as your own — for an upfront fee and ongoing royalties.

Some of America's best known businesses are franchises, including McDonald's, Burger King, Midas Mufflers, Budget Rent-a-Car, Ramada Inns, and so on. Many lesser known businesses are franchised as well.

The advantage of a franchise is that you get the benefit of someone else's experience and marketing clout in opening your own business. The disadvantage is that you don't have much leeway in operating or promoting the business as you see fit. Therefore, franchises tend to be best for individuals who don't have a great desire to be creative or individualistic in their own business.

Franchising has been an area of tremendous business growth, and therefore deserving of at least some of your initial attention. Many books and articles are available on the subject.

■ Conclusion: The Power of the Idea

The idea-generation process is probably the least well understood part of the business start-up process. We don't understand it well because it is a creative process, and creativity is an area that is as much speculation as fact. Unfortunately, though, the idea is key to business success, so we must use what we do know as effectively as possible. Here are three points essential to keep in mind as you come up with and evaluate ideas:

1. Good ideas are a dime a dozen. If you talk with successful entrepreneurs, you quickly find that they are overflowing with ideas for new businesses. But they know there is no way they can possibly implement many of them, nor would they want to. They realize that coming up with an idea and implementing it are totally different tasks.

The challenge you face is not just finding an idea but selecting from among the many ideas you come across to find the one that is right for you. The process is a weeding or winnowing process. You review ideas that come up, discard those that don't fit your needs, and keep those you want. Those that are left get more serious consideration, using the suggestions described previously.

2. Idea evaluation is a complex process. Because you likely have lots of ideas, you may feel as if you are at loose ends. How can you make sense of so many different ideas? It's essential to be able to evaluate ideas objectively and dispassionately. That process is not easy, but it can be done. A process is described in Exercise I at the end of this chapter.

3. It's easy to fall in love with an idea. It's especially easy if you are unhappy in your job or unemployed. The lure of the idea that will help you escape your current predicament is particularly strong. I know an engineer who was unhappy in his job as a college professor and decided that the way out was to start a consulting business specializing in evaluating environmental problems. Unfortunately, his idea was driven so strongly by his desire to start a new career that he didn't do a realistic enough evaluation of his idea. If he had, he would have determined that, while he had engineering expertise, he didn't have the necessary knowledge base, including familiarity with governmental funding trends and industry efforts to comply with new regulations. Within a year, his business had folded and he was back to teaching.

■ **Exercise 1: Idea-Crunching**

To help you avoid the fate of the professor, I have constructed an exercise to thoroughly evaluate your idea. Each time you come up with an idea for a new business, go through this sequence of questions. When you find yourself unable to provide a full answer or your answer is troublesome, you have a potential problem. Think about how you might resolve it.

1. **Summarize your business idea in fifty words or less.**

2. **As specifically as possible, identify the source of your idea (i.e., from work experience, long observation of an industry, a business publication).**

3. **List the questions you need answered about the industry/field before you can implement the idea. (No matter how familiar you are with the industry, you should need some additional information. Conversely, if your information needs are very broad or fundamental, you should question the idea.)**

4. **Identify three other examples of your idea being used. If you can't, name three obstacles that are preventing the idea from being implemented and explain how you will overcome them.**

5. **Identify three ways in which your idea is an improvement over other approaches being used.**

6. **How long have you had this idea? If less than three months, explain why you shouldn't give the idea more time to settle.**

7. Are you ready to commit to this idea for the next five years? Why or why not?

8. Is your idea for a product or a business? If it is based on one product, explain how the product will lead to a business.

9. Are you the best person to implement this idea? If yes, provide three reasons to back up your claim.

10. Very roughly, what level of sales and profits could this business achieve in two years? Do these estimates justify the risk you will be taking in starting a business?

■ Exercise II: Followup Assessment

If you have passed the previous test, put your idea to some additional tests as follows:

1. What are your two most important personal goals over the next five years?

2. How will this business idea help you achieve these personal goals?

3. Describe your market niche in fifty words or less.

4. List three qualifications you have to pursue a business in this market.

TESTING THE IDEA

"Listening to your customers is a way to make a fortune."

. . . .

Mo Siegel, Celestial Seasonings

When you talk about testing your business idea, you are really talking about doing market research. But when you mention the term market research to entrepreneurs, you invariably delve into an area about which there is strong disagreement.

"In the food business, the entrepreneur who is going to hang his or her hat on market research will be bankrupt within two months," says David Liederman of David's Cookies.

However, George Kachajian of Silicon Technology Corp. believes, "Market research is a critical part of any new business."

Frank Carney, the founder of Pizza Hut, is skeptical: "I have seen companies go out and design products and put up test facilities and do all that. That doesn't ensure their success any more than if they just went out and opened up."

Why would successful entrepreneurs differ so strongly about a subject as seemingly straightforward as market research? Part of the problem appears to be confusion over what is meant by market research. Liederman suggests that market research is some academic exercise removed from reality. Carney implies that market research means establishing a fancy test site that is somehow different from what would be established in real life.

Yet market research isn't limited to abstract data and statistics any more than it is limited to fancy test sites. If you discuss an idea for a business or a product with friends, family, or potential customers, you are conducting a basic kind of market research. Market research encompasses many different tasks, all of which boil down to *determining whether enough potential customers exist for your product or service and, if so, whether they will buy from you.*

These tasks include the following:

- Accumulating statistics on the number of potential customers.
- Conducting a written or telephone survey of potential customers to determine whether they would use your product or service.
- Performing in-depth interviews of potential customers to determine their likes and dislikes concerning your product or service.
- Obtaining industry information from a trade association.
- Attending a trade show to learn about the attitudes and behavior of potential customers and competitors.
- Plugging into a data base to assemble magazine and newspaper articles that have been written about your product or service category and industry over the last year.
- Gathering information about competitors.
- Making a prototype of your product or service and trying it out on potential customers.
- Handing out samples of your product and determining user reactions.
- Opening a store, sending out catalogs, or otherwise beginning the business to determine the viability of your idea.

This list could be significantly expanded because market research encompasses many different actions. Not every successful entrepreneur will have gone through every single action that may be considered market research. But every successful entrepreneur — including those who disparage market research — will have used at least a few of these techniques.

One way to look at market research is as insurance. The more you do, the more likely you are to come up with important information that could save a serious mistake later in your new company's life. In today's increasingly turbulent business world, the more insurance you can obtain, the better.

This chapter examines in greater detail some of the more useful approaches applied by successful entrepreneurs to test their products or services early on. As was the situation in the previous chapter about how successful entrepreneurs came up with their ideas, there is often more going on than even the successful entrepreneurs realize.

■ Gaining Knowledge

Most successful entrepreneurs will tell you that they didn't go in for a lot of tedious library-type research. Rather, they say, they just went out and did it. They started up a business and saw how things went. That's certainly what David Liederman implies as he pooh-poohs market research.

When you begin probing what was really going on, though, you get a different perspective. You realize, as I described in the first chapter, that a fairly complex process is involved. Much of that process is rooted in the work experiences the entrepreneurs had before starting their companies — experiences that enabled the entrepreneurs to gain essential knowledge.

When first asked about market research, David Liederman describes a rather primitive approach: "I had my brother and my wife and the woman I wrote my cookbook with and my mother test the cookies. And we ate the cookies, we played with the recipes a little bit — more butter, less butter, more chocolate, less chocolate — and when they liked them, I sold the cookies. That was my market research."

That wasn't all, however. Liederman also had many years in the food business — first as a chef and then starting and running his sauce business. So he knew how the industry was structured, how the distribution chain worked, which niches had heavy competition, and so forth.

But that wasn't the end of the story. Two years elapsed between the time in 1977 when he walked into the Berkeley cookie store and "found religion" and when he opened his first store. Those two years were spent planning his business (a task described in more detail in Chapter 8) and presumably doing what I would interpret as market research. What he was accomplishing with his cookie experiments and planning efforts was filling in gaps in his knowledge and experience so he would be prepared when he opened for business.

Even given his food background and planning efforts, Liederman almost didn't succeed. During the first two months after he opened his first store in midtown Manhattan in June 1979, "People came by and said the cookies are ugly. . . . And they said the store looks like a urinal. We were going broke."

He was saved by a *New York Times* cookie-tasting contest in which David's Cookies scored well. "That was just in time, because I couldn't pay the August rent. Suddenly, people who were saying the cookies were ugly were standing in line to buy our cookies. . . . I definitely was lucky." Indeed, if the *New York Times* hadn't come along, Liederman might have been a victim of insufficient market research.

■ Gathering Data

Christine Martindale of Esprit Miami describes a similar approach to market research before opening her flower-distribution company. She used her experience and knowledge to gather information essential to testing her idea.

"The only real job I had as an adult was in the flower business. When I began working in the flower business [in 1971], it was just a young business. People had just started importing flowers at that time. . . . There were a lot of little farms springing up in Bogota that had no outlet for their flowers in Miami. They needed a market to ship the flowers through, so the opportunity existed. So I just opened up. I went to Colombia. I didn't know how to negotiate. I didn't know how to bargain."

But when pressed, she acknowledges that more was going on. "I knew from my experience in the business that concentration of customers was predominantly on the East Coast. There are 400 or 800 wholesalers in the United States, and the importers in Miami were only selling to about 200 of those, and they were all selling to the same 200. . . .There were customers out there that were not being serviced."

And how did Martindale make such a fundamental but key discovery? "It was just experience in the business. I went to the *Yellow Pages*. I went to the library and made copies of the *Yellow Pages* of wholesalers in every city, and I started calling and told them who I was and what I was doing and how I could get them flowers. I had to investigate how to transport them."

What kind of market research process are we seeing, and how can would-be entrepreneurs emulate it? Both Liederman and Martindale did fairly sophisticated market research, but it was on-the-job market research. It was research done over a number of years based on experience in their industry or a related industry.

I question whether a would-be entrepreneur with little or no experience in the flower industry could have grasped the opportunity that sat waiting to be exploited, even after days or weeks in the library and in contact with industry trade associations. The observations and conclusions Martindale was able to make might have been possible only for someone actually immersed in the business.

Taking her experience a step further, though, it becomes clear how important seemingly simple tools can become in providing critical data. Because Martindale knew exactly what she was searching for, she was able to use a source as basic as *Yellow Pages* from cities around the country to gather the names of prospective customers.

■ Talking to Prospective Customers

There are two ways to gauge the reactions of prospective customers:

1. *Do a survey.* This requires constructing a questionnaire, locating prospective customers, and getting their answers to the questions (typically by telephone or by a mailed questionnaire). Some major corporations even conduct these kinds of surveys in supermarkets or shopping centers. With some representative sampling of several hundred prospects, it is possible to draw conclusions about what they want or don't want. Unfortunately, this is an expensive and time-consuming approach that most entrepreneurs have neither the money nor the patience for.

2. *Conduct interviews.* Getting several prospective customers together in a group for an hour or two to probe their feelings about a particular product or service is referred to in marketing jargon as a focus group. The information is more qualitative than quantitative. That is, you get a sense of attitudes and feelings, but the information is not statistically reliable. Variations on the focus-group format include interviews with individual prospects, consultations with suppliers and industry experts, and discussions at trade shows with customers and prospects.

Most successful entrepreneurs use the second approach. They try to compensate for the absence of statistically meaningful responses by honing their antennas carefully as people respond to questions and ideas. As Mo Siegel observes: "If you make something and your friends say they like it, you can see if they are sincere or just patronizing you. If a lot of people tell you that they like it, it is somewhat of an indication. If you don't have money to test, keeping your ears open and listening can make up for a lot."

After George Kachajian's experience with the unsafe silicon-slicing machine had stimulated his idea for an improved version, "I discussed it with several people, some of my customers, and I found that a company in Fitchburg, Massachusetts, had been in the saw business of the horizontal and vertical blade. A couple of weeks after the accident, I was up in Fitchburg." There, he confirmed that his idea was feasible and began mapping out ways to make the new product.

When Jim Lowry considered leaving a large consulting firm to start his own, he asked some of his existing clients whether they might switch to him in his new firm. "I knew that the clients that I had been serving were more loyal to me as a professional than to my firm. So once you know that and test the waters, don't be bashful — ask them. This is your life. You say, 'Hey, if I leave on Monday, would you give me business? Would you give me a contract?' If they say no, I would think twice about it. But if all of them say, 'Yes, we will definitely give you a contract,' sort of discount it. Probably only two of them will come through. Not all five of them will come through, but two of them will, and this will be enough to get you started."

■ Researching the Competition

If there is one area in which successful entrepreneurs agree that academic-type research can be useful, it is competitive information. They all feel that it is essential to know as much about the competition as possible, and the best place to get that — aside from on-site observations — is at libraries, through electronic data bases, and from literature put out by competitors.

Too often, they point out, would-be entrepreneurs don't take the competition as seriously as they should. According to Frank Carney, "If you don't know your competitor or you think light of your competitor, which is very typical for an entrepreneur," then trouble is brewing. Would-be entrepreneurs "say they can do it much better and they don't even study the competitor. There is a reason the competitor has a business and you had better find out what it is and what is going to make those customers come to your store instead of his."

Lowry is adamant on this point: "I say analyze your competitors and analyze them to death. It is surprising how much material and data is available to the average person if he or she really seeks it. You can find out about the competition by merely going to the library. There is a lot of information about markets, about industries, about individual firms. You don't have to invest a lot of your own money. The books are there — *Standard & Poors, Dun & Bradstreet,* all these journals that have been used by the major corporations for years and years are there for the average businessperson who wants to start a business. Use them."

The key issue concerning competition is how you stack up, he notes. "The number one thing is providing a product or service that your customer will like better than your competition, so I think that you always keep your eye on the client or customer."

Mo Siegel goes a step further. In assessing the competition, he advises: "Look at all of their product literature, service literature, and figure out what they are doing that is so good and adapt it to your own way of doing something. There is no reason to reinvent the wheel. If someone has done a good job and you are competing with him, use the

FREE GOVERNMENT ASSISTANCE

The federal government can be of important assistance in your market research efforts. As several of the entrepreneurs interviewed noted, the government generates a tremendous amount of census, labor, and other data.

The government also provides services that assist and guide entrepreneurs in doing worthwhile market research. The U.S. Small Business Administration (SBA) sponsors several programs designed specifically to aid start-up entrepreneurs in market planning and research.

The most prominent SBA programs are the Small Business Development Centers (SBDC) and Small Business Institutes (SBI). These are mainly university-based centers that make available business school professors and graduate students to answer questions and guide entrepreneurs in their market research. In some cases, the SBDC or SBI will provide students to help conduct surveys and other research.

Call your local SBA office for the SBDC or SBI nearest you.

best of his ideas and a few of your own."

In an increasing number of industries, franchises and huge chains of supermarket-type stores have achieved tremendous power. Once-stable businesses like dry cleaning establishments, hardware stores, and stationery stores now face serious competition from franchises and/or chains.

It is essential that you be aware of the existence of such competitors, even if they haven't yet opened in your region. In looking over articles and data-base material, be alert to the names of major players or fast-growing companies that are mentioned. Research each one as much as possible. In the case of franchises, play the role of potential franchisee, calling the company to obtain literature it uses to sell individuals on buying a franchise. You will learn important data about the franchise as well as industry trends.

You want to avoid opening a new retail establishment and then waking up one morning to find a franchise or chain outlet opening down the street.

■ Testing a Prototype

A prototype of a product or service is a trial version — a single model or small batch of product or an experimental version of a service. When David Liederman and Mo Siegel asked friends and relatives to try samples of cookie and tea products, the entrepreneurs were testing a prototype. They were trying a version of the product out on potential customers.

Prototypes become more important as the expense of the product or service rises. The last thing a new company with a $10,000 or $20,000 product wants to encounter is a serious flaw or customer complaint after some hundreds or thousands of the product have been produced.

Thus for George Kachajian's silicon-slicing machine, which would sell for between $20,000 and $30,000, a prototype was mandatory. "What we did was build a prototype machine, and then we invited customers to go to [the assembly plant] and look at it and give us their critique and comments. In this case, RCA came up from Mountaintop, Pennsylvania, and looked at the equipment and said it was fine and made some suggestions that we implemented."

■ Establishing the Right Price

This is perhaps the trickiest part of any market research. Pricing is never easy, even for established corporations with lots of money to spend on complicated surveys. Most fundamentally, though, pricing is a function of two factors:

1. Your costs.
2. What the competition is charging.

Using these two factors, it's possible to come up with several pricing approaches:

• *The undercut-the-competition approach.* Would-be entrepreneurs often fall into the trap of spending lots of time and money adding value to a product or service, only to underprice it so as to undercut the competition. The danger in this strategy is twofold: your price won't allow you to make an adequate profit and potential customers may perceive your product or service to be of questionable quality because of the low price.

This isn't to say that it isn't compelling at times and can't work, especially for a service firm in which the principal cost is the founder's labor. Betsy Tabak of Tabak and Associates, a Cleveland marketing communications firm, recalls: "I did underprice my services when I started the business, and I did it on purpose. I wanted to be able to get experience. I wanted to develop a track record. And I wanted to sell what I have to sell, probably at any cost. It was so important to get started, to get some visibility."

• *The value approach.* For a product company that is able to keep its costs down, the price determinant can be what some entrepreneurs refer to as value. Here is how Gordon Segal explains it in regard to Crate & Barrel's approach: "To establish value, you have to see what the competitive prices are in the marketplace. . . . If a glass sells for $5 in the marketplace and you are selling it for $3, you have established the value and you are able to say to the consumer, 'Our prices are of a better value. They are not discounted, they are not cheaper, we just import directly and consequently have better value.' "

• **The fake-the-competition approach.** A shrewd assessment of pricing strategy is offered by George Kachajian in introducing his new silicon-slicing machines during the early 1970s. "Our original costs were in the area of $14,000 [per machine] and...my competitors were up in the area of $24,000 for a machine. . . . From a marketing point of view, if I put in a high price, I get my competitors to relax and look upon me as no competition. So I put my price at $28,250, $4,000 above the nearest competition. And that kind of lulled them to sleep, so they raised their prices to come up to mine. When I got my manufacturing in place, I dropped from $28,250 to $21,250 and killed them."

Clearly, then, there is no single way to establish prices. The better you understand the marketplace, the more easily you will be able to come up with a pricing approach that will work best for your new company.

■ Opening for Business

For many successful entrepreneurs, the real test marketing comes when they open their doors to customers. That was the approach used by Pizza Hut. According to Frank Carney: "We had a lot of friends and a lot of personal contacts, because we grew up in Wichita and went to school there, so we knew that our friends would come in and try it. But we didn't do any extensive testing. The day before we opened, we gave away pizza and I remember my brother got a little upset, but it was my idea to give it away and we gave away so much, we didn't have any money to buy ingredients for the next day of operation." (The ingredients were found at the family grocery.)

A similar tale comes from Gordon Segal in recounting Crate & Barrel's beginnings. Indeed, the little market research he did yielded some negative results. "When we opened the doors, we were totally basing it on our feelings that what we were bringing to the market-place would create a customer base that was there. We thought that there was a customer base there, but there was no test. We were too small to test. We talked to friends and actually, most people we talked to were discouraging about what we were doing and about where we were going to open our first store. Those people said it wouldn't work."

But he decided to buck the prevailing wisdom. "I think we went into it with the knowledge that we had to have the ability to go and buy direct from Europe and in a sense do something different from everyone else who had tried to do this in the past. When I say we wanted to do it differently, we meant that not only could we bring better design to the marketplace, we truly believed because of the way we would structure the distribution that we would go and find factories that weren't already flooding the marketplace, find product for a Chicago consumer that wasn't already in the marketplace."

In retrospect, he concludes: "We didn't go into it in a very professional manner at all. We went into it like two enthusiastic young people who have an idea and want to sell that idea to consumers. And that was to bring good design to your tabletop."

■ Listening to Customers

No entrepreneur can expect to get everything right from the beginning. There must be adjustments in approach and strategy. Most entrepreneurs refer to it as listening to the customer. That can be difficult, as Gordon Segal recalls: "You have to absolutely adjust to what the customer really wants. I remember years ago that we brought in demi cups and saucers for espresso, and there was no market for them. We kept on saying there is lots of market for them. We kept big gigantic breakfast cups for tea. But there was no market for them, either. Europe had a great market for them. So you can go bankrupt if you don't listen to the customer. You can't just do what you want and what you feel. You have to eventually blend it with what the customer wants. So you have to constantly modify."

Frank Carney also learned quickly the lesson of not only listening closely to customers but of acting on that information. "After the business gets going, you can see what the customers like. And so one of the favorite pizzas was pepperoni pizza and sausage pizza. When people were confused about what to order, we would say, 'Most people order pepperoni or sausage pizza, and we suggest you try one of them.' That would actually help people make their decisions when we first started."

A big part of the constant adjustment is improving quality. All successful entrepreneurs agree on the importance of providing the highest quality product or service at the lowest possible price. A key part of the process of listening to customers is determining what they mean by high quality. David Liederman sees it as fairly straightforward: "If you put good stuff into a recipe, if you buy the best — butter, nuts, chocolate — and put it into a recipe, mix it intelligently, and sell it fresh, people are going to buy it as long as there is value for the money."

■ Your Market Research Program

How do you actually go about doing the most useful and cost-effective market research? The revelations presented earlier in this chapter by successful entrepreneurs provide useful insights, but it is important to have an overall approach that will work for you. Here are some suggestions for putting together your own program:

- **Gather more data than you need.** Even if you have extensive knowledge of and experience in the industry in which you want to start a business, be sure to do research. That usually means heading to a public library or possibly a business school library.

  Whatever source you use, don't be afraid to ask for help, advises James Lowry. "Go to the people in charge of the business section of the library. They will lean over backwards to help you. They will do all kinds of computer searches to help you in terms of competition. . . . The other thing we relied very heavily on is the U.S. Census. It has a mammoth amount of information on businesses, on trends, on percentages of work that goes to entrepreneurs and firms doing business with the government, the private sector. . . . There is a lot of information available and it does not cost a lot of money."

- **Look at the big picture.** In today's information-flooded society, it's easy to feel as if you're drowning in data. Some have referred to the feeling as information overload.

  You should be prepared, once you've gathered data, to analyze it closely, says Lowry. "I think you have to stand back and say, 'What does this tell me, does it tell a story? First, does it tell me that there is a market and second, does it tell me that there is competition and what the nature of the competition is? Last, does it tell me I can make money in it?' "

  The first question he raises is the most basic, and most easily overlooked. If you are considering starting a business that sells public relations services for biotechnology firms in the Northwest, you first need to determine whether there are enough prospective companies to provide the necessary volume. Keep in mind that if you find there are a hundred such companies, you can expect to capture some small percentage as customers.

  If you have doubts about whether the market is really large enough, consider whether there are similar companies you could market to, like pharmaceutical firms or medical laboratories.

Entrepreneurs planning retail businesses need to study the demographics of the shopping area in which they are operating. Some of that information may be available from local and federal population figures, but it may be necessary to simply hang around the area you are considering locating in and count the number of shoppers at different times of the day.

- **Write down your findings.** As you do your library research and bump up against information overload, try to keep notes about the key issues you must consider. This information involves the questions posed earlier in this chapter as well as those particular to the industry, location, product, or service you have chosen. If you are adept with a computer, maintain your findings in a data base program, arranged according to people, sources, and other input.

- **Keep a flow of up-to-date information coming in.** In today's fast-changing world, yesterday's knowledge and information can quickly be outdated. Just because you worked in the health-food business or office-supply business two years ago doesn't mean there haven't been significant changes.

   Indeed, someone who worked in the office-supply business a few years back and had gone into some other business in the meantime might be stunned at the changes that took place in a very short time in terms of retailing approaches, mail-order efforts, and other distribution issues.

   It's important to monitor publications of your potential industry. But you should also monitor magazine and newspaper articles by using a computerized data base service. (See box on page 48 for further details.)

- **Ask the right questions.** Earlier in this chapter, I described the two main approaches to having customer prospects test your idea: a questionnaire approach and an interview approach. A key aspect of using either approach is coming up with the right questions. It's not just a matter of asking whether prospects would use your product or not.

The task of constructing questionnaires and focus groups can be quite complex and is the subject of many volumes in and of itself. There are issues of length, types of questions, incentives for participating, and so forth. But a few rules can help in putting your own queries together.

For a questionnaire being sent to many people, try to keep your questions as specific and the questionnaire as brief as possible. To keep it specific, concentrate on either yes/no answers or multiple-choice answers. Because you want to be able to tabulate the results, such answers will provide consistent feedback that will illustrate trends and preferences.

If you were contemplating starting a gourmet catering business, for example, you might survey corporate-event planners about how frequently they had used catering services in the last year (less than twice, two to four times, more than four times); how many times they planned to use such a service in the coming year; whether they preferred a hotel, banquet hall, restaurant, or in-house service; and so on.

For a focus group, keep your questions open ended but easy to answer. Thus, good questions for prospective customers of a new hair-cutting salon might be, "What bothers you most about the hair-cutting salon you use now?"; "What is the single most important feature you would like to see in a new hair salon?"; and "How important is price in your selection process?"

In a focus group, you are most interested in the overall tone, strength of opinions about particular subjects, and suggestions for features or improvements. Such a setting gives you a feeling about the prospective customer's mind-set.

Similarly, if you are interviewing suppliers or industry analysts, try to get their views by inquiring into the most significant problems, opportunities, and accomplishments in the industry.

That way, you get into their strongest feelings, about which they will talk most and which are usually the most important.

• **Don't take all feedback literally.** One of the most difficult things about questionnaires and interviews is interpreting what they mean. A corporate-events planner might tell a catering service that he or she feels that flower centerpieces are an unnecessary extravagance. But if a caterer neglects to include them at a party and senior executives of a company complain to the planner, you know how the planner is going to feel about the caterer.

Similarly, keep in mind that it's impossible with any product

---

THE GREAT EQUALIZER

Sophisticated market research used to be the province of major corporations.

Now, thanks to the power of computerized data bases, it's possible for individual entrepreneurs to quickly obtain important information about the marketplace. These data bases make it possible to locate and access comprehensive market studies, patents, scientific articles, data about competitors, and other sensitive information.

Some of these data bases can be reached via popular personal computer services like CompuServe and Prodigy. Others require specialized knowledge of computer commands and software.

In some cases, a librarian at your town or city library will be able to locate what you need at nominal fees. If not, the librarian can probably refer you to a consultant who specializes in accessing such data bases for an hourly fee. The computer data base services also charge fees based on the amount of time one spends sorting through material and the number of items provided.

It's possible to conduct a fairly comprehensive data search for a few hundred dollars for both a consultant and the data base—for information that not too many years ago would have taken months and cost many thousands of dollars to obtain.

or service to provide all the features and preferences that each and every prospective customer would like. The entrepreneur about to open a fitness center may find a few prospects who would like squash courts. But because they are so expensive to build, the entrepreneur would be correct to question their overall value to the business if they attract only a handful of members.

- **Assess the impact of more intense competition.** It's safe to assume that if your business shows signs of strong success, you will quickly have one or more competitors trying to imitate your success. Indeed, competition springs up more quickly and from more sources than ever before. Therefore, it is important that your market research takes into account what happens to your business if new competition suddenly springs up.

  There is no sure way to map out in advance how you might react. But it is worthwhile in any surveys or focus groups to ask what attributes or features of your product or service would be most important for maintaining customer loyalty. It is also useful in analyzing articles and conducting interviews with industry experts to determine the effects of intense competition in other geographic areas or in related industries.

  Also, from your research you should have some ideas about which additional features or services might most help your business. Be prepared to add those features or services as appropriate to stem the effects of competition.

- **Test your product or service before opening for business.** In the mail-order business, it is routine for new businesses to test a catalog or newsletter concept by sending out a representative mailing in small quantities to prospects. The results provide additional insights about potential customer interest. Most significantly, such a test enables the entrepreneur to abort the business before actual launch at much lower cost than if the business started full tilt.

Testing is certainly easier in the mail-order business than in the retail or manufacturing area, but even in those areas, it's possible. For instance, a woman planning to open an Indian-jewelry store might try first to sell jewelry at small house parties in the area in which the store would operate to determine market interest. Or before opening a business to manufacture upscale potato chips, it makes sense to subcontract the production out for a few small batches and determine receptivity of distributors and retailers.

Ultimately, the more you can test beforehand, the more confident you will be and the more likely you will be doing more things right than wrong.

• **Test promotional efforts.** At the same time that you are testing your product or service, take a shot at getting some publicity. You may want to send a news release to the local newspaper or an industry magazine to see if you can get the media to take notice of you. Once an article appears, you will have further information about how publicity might benefit your sales.

Remember, the name of the game is to gather as much information as possible and use that information to project accurately whether your idea is sound and if so how its success can be maximized. Keep in mind also that market research isn't a one-shot affair. Once you open for business, you should continuously collect information about customer likes and dislikes and adjust your business accordingly.

■ Exercise 1: Data Sources

For each of the following categories, list two potential resources by name (with location and phone number) who can provide you with information for and/or reaction to your business idea.

• **Bankers**

• **Trade associations**

• **Business associations**

• **Successful entrepreneurs**

• **Professional market research groups**

• **Suppliers**

• **Data base**

• **Accountants**

■ Exercise II: Using Your Research

1. Identify your three most important groups of potential customers, defining them by the criteria you believe are most relevant (age, demographics, industry, etc.).

2. Name your three most important competitors, and describe briefly the single factor that makes each most dangerous to your new business.

3. Describe in two or three sentences how your prospective customers feel about each competitor.

4. Describe briefly the two factors or issues that are likeliest to help make your business attract customers from each of the three competitors.

5. Where did the information for the answers to the previous two questions come from (your own interviews of prospects, media articles, an industry market study)?

■ Exercise III: Pricing

1. Provide calculations for two or three possible prices for your product or service.

2. List your most significant competitor's prices.

3. If your prices are higher, why are they higher and how will you justify them to prospective customers?

4. If your prices are lower, why are they lower and how will they help you attract prospective customers?

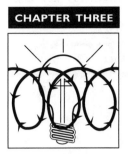

PROTECTING THE IDEA

"If your product is good, there will be people there copying it."

. . . .

Frank Carney, founder of Pizza Hut

In my experience, the matter of protecting a new-business idea is one of the most anxiety-provoking issues confronting start-up entrepreneurs. I know entrepreneurs who refuse to discuss their ideas in anything but the most general terms — even with relatives or close friends — for fear that someone will rush in to use the idea and make millions doing it.

Unfortunately, such secrecy doesn't work well if you take the advice I offered in the previous chapter of trying to get as much feedback and reaction as possible to your idea. The more you try your idea out on other people, the farther you spread it around and risk that someone else will use it.

So what are your options?

■ Less Danger Than You Imagine

The fact is, there's no one right way to protect your idea. My personal opinion, based on many years of observing and working with entrepreneurs, is that they usually don't have as much to fear as they think about losing their ideas to predators.

Consider your own reaction to hearing an idea for a new business. Chances are your daily life is pretty busy, what with earning a living, tending to your family, taking care of your household chores, and doing the 101 other things that are part of getting through each week. Besides, you are likely exposed to all kinds of ideas, not only for new businesses but for buying stocks, consumer products, insurance, and so forth that the media, salespeople, friends, acquaintances, and family members throw your way.

If you are like most people, you are probably fairly skeptical of the new ideas you hear about. Good ideas, as I suggested in Chapter 1, are a dime a dozen. How many do you really act upon? How many do you have *time* to act upon?

The reality is that most people you discuss your business idea with won't immediately appreciate how brilliant it is simply because their initial reaction is one of skepticism. And even if they did see its brilliance, chances are they wouldn't be inclined to devote the time and energy necessary to implement it. As noted in Chapter 1, it can take several years of very hard work before one even begins to achieve success. Most people are simply too busy running their own lives to devote several years to trying out your idea.

■ Striking the Right Balance

Having said all that, I don't mean to suggest that you should ignore the matter of protection. Indeed, there are probably some lawyers who would be uncomfortable with what I've said already. These lawyers specialize in what has come to be known as intellectual property. Simply stated, intellectual property is the valuable ideas, information, and concepts that lead to products, services, and orders. Intellectual property can be as important as traditional property like real estate and machinery. But because intellectual property tends to be carried around in your head, sketched on paper, or stored in computers, its value often isn't as immediately apparent as it should be, even to those most closely involved in its creation.

As our society becomes increasingly knowledge driven, intellectual property takes on ever-increasing significance. Many lawyers and entire law firms now specialize in matters of intellectual property and such protection methods as patents, trademarks, and copyrights (which are discussed later in this chapter). These lawyers obviously feel strongly that entrepreneurs should exercise great care in protecting their intellectual property, and they can point to an increasing number of real cases to prove their points. There are cases of computer software entrepreneurs who have lost their rights to exciting new products because, unknown to the entrepreneurs, free-lance programmers who don't sign an appropriately worded agreement may have copyrights on material they create. And there are cases of employees running off with prospect and customer lists from young businesses and starting up on their own.

I would not disagree with these lawyers. Indeed, as a writer, I have sought out and benefited from legal ways to protect my own intellectual property. And I strongly believe that entrepreneurs should know their legal options and take all necessary steps to protect themselves. It is simply too easy to inadvertently give away intellectual property that might have been protected had the correct legal steps been taken.

I want to emphasize that entrepreneurs should have the right attitude and priorities regarding protecting their ideas. The most brilliant idea in the world is worthless if you are so worried about it being taken that you shy away from testing it appropriately and fully. Even the most brilliant ideas will need to be altered in important ways before they can be turned into successful businesses. And the only way to determine how is to do the necessary market testing, which entails some leap of faith about letting others in on important aspects of the idea.

Moreover, even if you take extensive legal action to protect yourself, remember that there is no such thing as absolute protection. Even that seemingly strongest of legal protective devices — the patent

— is only as good as your ability to protect it. One entrepreneur I know who has received many patents makes the observation that a patent is merely "a ticket of admission" to court to protect yourself from possible infringement. It may mean little if you don't have the thousands of dollars necessary to sustain a long legal battle — and how many start-up entrepreneurs have such resources?

Frank Carney of Pizza Hut fame probably best articulates the attitude I am striving for: "A lot of people are paranoid about others stealing their ideas. In reality, if somebody wants to copy it, they can come very, very close. It doesn't make sense to spend a lot of money and time being overly concerned with protecting every single facet of your operation. You want to get the core of it to where you get a head start in the marketplace now. If your product is good, there will be people there copying it. Pizza Hut has been copied, McDonald's has been copied. It is going to happen, so don't get too concerned over it. That is, don't spend too much time worrying about it. It's much better to spend time worrying about the customer and whether you are making money and how you are going to grow the business."

■ What You Should Look Out For

My somewhat long-winded point, then, is that before becoming obsessed with the legalities of protecting your idea, you must first try to take a broad, practical view toward the issue of protecting your idea for a new business. Having made that point, I would note that in a number of circumstances, protection is an issue. For example:

• **The "exception."** Sure, most people don't have the time or inclination to steal your idea, but there are those occasional individuals who are perceptive enough to recognize a good idea when they hear one. Those individuals could well go out and steal your idea. I have heard of situations in which entrepreneurs have had their ideas copied by others before the originators could follow through on the ideas.

Keep in mind that just because someone uses your idea doesn't mean it's no longer of value to you. Chances are the copycat won't execute it the way you would have and, if it's a truly good idea (i.e., there are lots of potential customers), then who's to say you can't still start the business? More often than not, there's room for more than one of any type of business. And in the meantime, you can watch your imitator so as to gain insights into what he or she is doing right and wrong, and use that information to help you refine and improve the idea.

If your idea was somehow protected legally, it may be that you can go after the culprit. For instance, if the person used a name you had trademarked, you could force him or her to stop using that name.

- **The invention.** Some business ideas are the result of proprietary technology or specialized knowledge that lends itself to being patented. To let the idea out before you have completely formulated and tested it technically — especially to those with similar training or background — could invite imitation. If the invention could lead to foreign sales, you should investigate filing for overseas patents as quickly as possible, since patents in most European and Asian countries are awarded according to who was first to apply. In the United States, you must file within a year of disclosing details of the invention; in the case of overlapping applications, awards are made based on a judgment by patent officials of who was the first to conceive the invention.

  The bottom line is that in this situation, entrepreneurs should be careful not to broadcast too many details before they have determined what their legal rights are and have taken the appropriate precautions.

- **The advanced-stage idea.** Generally speaking, the further along you are in developing your idea and the greater the number of indications of success you've had, the more vulnerable you are to

57

losing your idea to an imitator. If you are already at the prototype stage and are getting favorable reactions from prospective customers, then you are more vulnerable to rip-off than if you have just thought something up and are discussing it at a cocktail party. That's because as you move along, you are turning the idea into something real. And as it becomes more real, it requires less imagination by potential copiers to envision. It's not unlike the difference between trying to sell a run-down old house with ugly wallpaper and a fixed-up version of the same house. The latter is much easier to get people excited about because they don't have to imagine how it will look. They can see it.

• **The first helpers.** In testing out your idea, you may hire one or more administrative assistants, production workers, or consultants to assist you in your market research. Those individuals will, of course, gain intimate knowledge of not only your idea but of how potential customers are reacting to it.

They may be so impressed with what you are doing and learning in your market research that they decide it's too attractive an opportunity to pass up — for themselves. Suddenly, instead of having several assistants, you have unforeseen competition.

This sort of situation can be dealt with legally by requiring everyone you bring on board to sign agreements related to their ability to compete with you or use information they obtain while working for you. The mechanics of doing this are discussed in more detail later in this chapter.

■ The Reality of Protection

Once you have the issue of protection in its proper perspective, you might ask, what sort of practical steps can I take to protect my idea? Before seeking to answer that question, be aware of two essential points about achieving protection of your business ideas:

• **Total protection is impossible.** An essential point about protecting your idea that I made earlier but that bears repeating is that it is impossible to gain total protection of any idea. You can only take precautions and put up roadblocks that discourage others from taking advantage of you.

An analogy is the challenge of protecting your house or apartment from burglary. You can take precautions like attaching timers to lights and radios and getting neighbors to take in your newspapers and water your lawn. You may even buy a sophisticated burglar alarm that hooks up with a security firm so that any break-in is reported to the police. But no matter how extensive your protective efforts, you cannot prevent professional burglars intent on breaking in from getting in. You can only deter them.

The same applies to protecting your idea. You can only deter potential poachers via appropriate barriers, legal and practical. And now, with intense international competition extending to nearly all products and services, the problem is global in nature. You have only to look at the major problem companies ranging from fashion (Pierre Cardin) to pharmaceuticals (Merck) have had with knockoff products to know how serious the challenge of protection is.

Christine Martindale, the founder of Esprit Miami, gained firsthand experience with the vagaries of international competition in her flower-importing business. She recalls that she worked with a flower grower (hybridizer) to develop a new variety and color of flower. "I did file a patent for a new variety of flower that was invented by the hybridizer. It took us three and a half years to get the patent, and by then everyone had stolen cuttings from the farms in Italy and in Colombia, and a lot of people had it. There is no way to collect royalties or stop growing once it is a common product."

• **Some ideas are easier to protect than others.** Generally speaking, the less unique your idea is, the more difficult it is to protect.

If you are planning to open a sandwich shop or a dress boutique, you will be able to obtain less in the way of legal protection than if you are starting a business marketing a new type of synthetic heart valve.

This isn't to say you can't achieve some sort of protection for a common type of business. Subway Sandwiches and Salads became a huge chain of sandwich stores, helped in part by a name that was protected by trademark. More easy to protect is a technological advance, such as instant film photography. However, as even Polaroid discovered during the early 1980s, actually protecting its technology against invasion from the likes of Kodak was a very costly and time-consuming venture.

The next few sections, then, are about deterrence. They are about the steps, legal and practical, that you can take to reduce the risk your idea will be used by others.

■ The Unique Value of You

For businesses of the more common variety, such as retail, wholesale, or many service businesses, the most important protection you have may be your own creativity and ingenuity. After all, this is what will primarily set your business apart from the many others already out there. Gordon Segal of Crate & Barrel describes this aspect of protection:

"I think what keeps a retailer from being copied is that a store is really an expression of that person's personality and his vision, and that in a sense can never be copied. You cannot copy an individual and, over more than twenty years, many people have tried to copy what we were doing because we were so successful and it looked so simple. And it is simple in concept. But how we execute, how we buy, what values we offer, the things we do are peculiar to our personality. . . . There are so many elements that make up that store, that make it unique, that it can never be exactly copied. A concept can be copied — a concept of a warehouse store or a discount store. But each one is individual. So we never got paranoid about competition. We never really got paranoid about copying."

David Liederman of David's Cookies has a similar attitude toward the issue of protection. When asked how he dealt with the issue of protecting his cookie recipes, he replied: "You cannot copyright a recipe. It is not even possible to trademark a recipe."

But, he noted, the cookie recipe is much more than a list of ingredients. "I could give you the recipe and you could go out and buy the ingredients, and it wouldn't taste anything like it tastes in the stores. That's because we buy fresher nuts and fresher chocolate. The key to doing a food business is to develop your sources of supply. That's where expertise comes in."

Liederman searched long and hard for his special supply sources that enable him to make a cookie with a taste and texture difficult to duplicate. Thanks to his own expertise and creativity, something as common as a chocolate-chip cookie becomes proprietary.

I can certainly vouch for Liederman's explanation. I recall that when Mrs. Fields' Cookies were all the rage, an acquaintance gave me a recipe she said was for the exact same cookie. It wasn't clear where the acquaintance got the recipe. In any case, I quickly made the cookies and, sure enough, they weren't quite up to Mrs. Fields' standards.

■ The People You Trust — And What You Tell Them

One of the best ways to protect your idea lies in the character of the person you are talking to or doing business with, be it a potential customer, supplier, investor, or someone you are trying to recruit as a manager or an employee. Check each person out as carefully as you can beforehand.

The checking usually involves getting a character reference about the person from someone you trust. Thus, you'd rather discuss potential production issues with a supplier recommended by a business associate rather than going through the *Yellow Pages* or a trade association. The business associate knows if the supplier keeps his or her word on basic matters of pricing, delivery, and quality. Such dependability usually extends to matters of confidentiality and ethics.

Still and all, there is nothing that says you have to tell each person you come into contact with every detail about your idea. David Liederman points out that only a handful of the hundreds of people associated with his cookie stores knew the entire recipe and his sources of supply. That is because he intentionally divulged only what was necessary to various people involved in his business.

Even at a company as huge and successful as Coca-Cola, the actual recipe for producing Coke remains one of the company's most closely guarded secrets. It is said that only two or three people know everything about how Coke is made.

The message is clear: When you discuss your problems and

INTELLECTUAL PROPERTY TERMINOLOGY

Copyright. A copyright is government protection to prevent a company's reports, presentations, slides, and even videos from being reproduced and distributed by someone else. While the form of the work is protected, the actual ideas are not. To protect your rights against innocent infringements and be able to collect possible financial damages, you may want to register your copyright with the U.S. Copyright Office, though this is not considered essential for protection.

Employment agreement. An agreement between a company and an employee that can cover salary, length of employment, and stock options as well as assign intellectual property created on the job to the company.

Noncompete agreement. Sets limits for employees about their ability to set up a competing business during the time of their employment and for some period after leaving a company.

Nondisclosure agreement. Sets limits on dissemination of information by individuals who have more than casual contact with a company and its operations, including employees, investors, bankers, consultants, and even plant visitors.

requirements with a potential supplier, tell him or her only what is essential to fill your needs. That may mean providing a brief overview of what your company will do, along with the specifications of what you will need produced. But other critical details—your plans for advertising and distributing your product, for example—need not be a subject of conversation. Similarly, when you are interviewing a potential salesperson, details about production and service can be left unstated until the person comes on board and it becomes clear that he or she needs additional information.

Dealing with a potential investor is more tricky. If you are trying to raise money, you will be approaching prospective backers who will want all the information they can get about your idea to determine if they should commit. Unless you are extremely fortunate and get

Patent. One of the most valuable forms of government protection for product inventions, chemical formulas, and manufacturing processes judged to be novel and unobvious. A patent gives the holder the right to exclude others from making, using, and selling the covered product or process— or to sell rights to the patent in exchange for royalties—for seventeen years.

Service mark. This includes a service company's word or symbol or combinations of both, which can become a valuable form of graphic identification. It can be registered with the U.S. Patent and Trademark Office to protect it from unauthorized use.

Trademark. This includes a product company's word or symbol or combinations of both, which can become a valuable form of graphic identification. It can be registered with the U.S. Patent and Trademark Office to protect it from unauthorized use.

Trade secret. Proprietary information or processes—considered novel—that provide a company with important long-term competitive advantages.

backing from the first investor you meet, you will inevitably meet up with those individuals I refer to as "tire kickers." These are venture capitalists and other investors who are simply trying to stay up to date on what's out in the marketplace — or about to come on the marketplace. They may even have backed a company that somehow competes with the idea you are proposing. So the information you convey could very well wind up being used in ways you would rather not see it used.

Unfortunately, there is no foolproof way around this problem. You may ask the investors to sign nondisclosure agreements (discussed in the next section) and you can inquire into their investment portfolios to determine if they have invested in a similar company. You can also ask around to determine if they are trustworthy. But the bottom line is that you are taking some risk when you divulge details of your idea to such individuals.

Clearly, if you plan to apply for a patent or if you are using some technical or other advance of a proprietary nature, don't reveal the details to such prospective investors. Usually, if you tell them that you can't go further in a product description because certain details are proprietary, the investors will understand. Of course, if they become serious about investing in your business, you will likely have to work out a legal arrangement under which you divulge key details of your idea so they can evaluate its merit.

■ Common Sense Legal Precautions

It should be clear by this point that you owe it to yourself early in your business start-up effort to speak with a lawyer who knows something about intellectual property. This is typically a lawyer who specializes in patents and trade secrets.

If you are already far along in the start-up process and have completed your incorporation, you should still seriously consider consulting with a knowledgeable lawyer. Some who specialize in intellectual property have begun doing intellectual property audits that involve examining your business to gain the maximum protection possible for product ideas, customer lists, special sales techniques, and other proprietary data.

If you aren't far enough along in development of your business idea to feel it necessary to speak with a lawyer, here are some common sense steps you should take as you develop the idea:

- **Keep track of important documents — and make sure others know you are keeping track of them.** This means taking basic steps like placing a number on the cover of each business plan before making it available to a potential lender or investor. This lets each reader know that you monitor the whereabouts of the plan, and it helps emphasize the warning displayed on each plan that it is not to be copied or otherwise duplicated or distributed without your permission.

   Similarly, use certified or registered mail to ensure you have proof that important documents sent to prospective distributors or manufacturers were received. Another technique is to have someone you know and trust witness the business plan before you send it off — and sign it or a statement saying he or she read the plan with the title and date you are sending off.

- **Label documents that are considered proprietary.** This can mean stamping "confidential" on lists of prospective customers or of principal suppliers. Some newsletter publishers have begun taking the precaution of noting on each page of their publications that the material is copyrighted and it is unlawful to make additional copies without permission. Such steps remind employees, customers, and others that you are well aware of your intellectual property rights and you are prepared to take action to enforce those rights as strongly as you can.

- **Use nondisclosure agreements.** These are legal documents that oblige people you are dealing with to refrain from revealing information you are providing them. Nondisclosure agreements can be applied to any number of things of potential value to the company, including business plans, marketing plans, machinery, lists of prospective customers, and building plans.

These agreements can also be applied to any number of people you are dealing with, including new employees, consultants, and prospective customers. I have been asked to sign nondisclosure agreements before touring the plants of companies I planned to write about.

Such agreements serve similar purposes as the labeling approach. First, they enable you to keep control who is looking at what. Second, they send a message to outsiders that you know how to protect yourself and aren't someone to be trifled with.

Talk with a lawyer about the actual circumstances in which you should use nondisclosure agreements. The exact language and provisions of the agreement should be drawn up by a lawyer.

• *Use appropriate additional agreements for those you employ.* As you hire people — on either a contract or permanent basis—have each sign an agreement that limits his or her ability to take valuable information from your company and later use it to compete with you. Typically, such agreements take the form of a nondisclosure agreement, a noncompete agreement, and/or an employment agreement. Sometimes, an agreement may include several elements. For example, an employment agreement that provides for an employee to be paid a certain salary for the next two years may also require that the employee not be able to establish a competing business for two years after leaving the company.

While nondisclosure agreements are usually fairly straightforward, noncompete and employment agreements can become very complicated. The U.S. judicial system has tended to be reluctant about limiting a person's rights to earn a living, as noncompete agreements tend to do.

The key to such agreements is reasonableness. You shouldn't make the agreement more binding in scope than was represented by the work the individual did for the company. For instance, if your business covers a fifty-mile area, you may want to limit a key employee who has been with the company for several years from competing with you within the same fifty-mile radius for two or three years in order for the agreement to be binding. But if your company is national in scope, you may have reason to prohibit competition in all fifty states for some period of time.

Employment agreements similarly get complicated in terms of who has obligations to whom in the event an employee leaves before the agreement has expired or if a company wants a person to leave before the agreement is up — not only in the area of intellectual property but in other areas as well. Once again, legal advice is advised.

• *Be careful what you promise.* Start-up entrepreneurs are sometimes quick to promise new employees that stock will be available sometime in the future or that salary increases will come quickly if the company begins to make money. The entrepreneur may forget the promise, but the employees usually don't, and some entrepreneurs have gotten themselves into serious trouble as a result, especially if the promise is alluded to in a letter or memo. Even if it isn't written down, it can become legally binding in some states, depending on the circumstances.

Moreover, such promises can even undermine or invalidate nondisclosure or noncompete agreements that have been signed. When you write a letter welcoming a new employee, consider having a lawyer review it to make sure you haven't inadvertently implied that the person will be kept on for many years or will receive stock or other inducements you don't intend to give.

■ Key Protection Options

Intellectual property isn't just something to be protected but also to be exploited as a competitive advantage. That is, you shouldn't simply try to keep others from copying your idea, as important as that may seem. You should also think about intellectual property as just that — a type of property or asset that has value in its own right.

The material in this section is a brief overview of intellectual property considerations, preparatory to consulting with a lawyer. I am not a lawyer and the material here and in subsequent sections should *not* be used as a substitute for consulting with a lawyer. In addition, matters of intellectual property can become highly technical, deserving of entire books in their own right.

For a brief primer of intellectual property terms, see the box on pages 62–63. Here are some considerations in assessing the potential usefulness of key legal forms of protection:

- **The power of the patent.** Patents tend to be the first type of protection many entrepreneurs think about in considering intellectual property. That may be because they are associated with inventions, some fairly spectacular, ranging from zippers to lasers to instant film photography to miracle drugs. But many less spectacular items are patented — more than 1,000 weekly — including obscure machinery and chemicals and even designs for uniforms and dresses.

    The obvious advantage of the patent is that it is equivalent to a government-assigned license to exclusivity for seventeen years. More practically, though, a patent can provide a company with a competitive edge. Because it has the power to limit competition, it can be extremely important in this age of ever-intensifying competition. For that reason, patents are considered very important by potential investors. Being able to limit competition improves a company's chances of being able to prosper and grow, in their estimation.

    And just because you or your company receive a patent doesn't mean you must produce what you patented to make money from it. It is possible also to license the patent to others who do the production and who will pay you a royalty for each item sold for the seventeen years of the patent.

• **The trade-secret option.** Some of a patent's advantages can also be construed as disadvantages. For instance, the fact that the government issues a patent means that the information it requires to justify a patent is open for anyone to examine. Therefore, all the details you provide to explain your invention are available to potential competitors once the patent has been issued. Competitors can then determine whether they can find a way to replicate your work without infringing on the patent (or even by infringing on it if they conclude that you can't or won't adequately defend it). In any case, if competitors respect the patent, at the end of seventeen years it is available for all to copy. And of course, some great ideas or business approaches just don't qualify for patents.

For these reasons and others, some entrepreneurs opt for the trade-secret option to protect their competitive advantages. Trade secrets have legal protection against disclosure for eternity, so long as the owner tries hard to keep them secret. They can also be licensed to other organizations. As noted earlier, Coca-Cola is a classic example of a company that has thrived for decades using the trade-secret option to protect and license its formula for producing Coke.

The main disadvantage of trade secrets is that you have no protection in the event someone duplicates your process or approach independently of you or your company. There are also fewer hard-and-fast rules than there are for patents, such as protection being given to the first to invent a product or device.

• **The hidden value — and danger — of trademarks.** The name you give a product, any symbols you attach, and the overall graphic appearance of the name and symbols can become a trademark. (The same items for a service are a service mark.)

If your company becomes successful, its trademark or service mark similarly takes on added value. Just think of the power of such trademarks as those associated with Walt Disney characters, beer companies, and major-league baseball teams. Those organizations use their trademarks to sell whatever related products they wish, including T-shirts, coffee mugs, and hats.

You gain ownership of a trademark simply by being the first to use it on goods you are selling. You gain ownership of a service mark by being the first to use it in advertising or promotion. Unfortunately, you may discover that while you thought you were the first to use a particular trademark, you weren't. If you inadvertently use a trademark that is similar to that being used by another company, you may find yourself in the awkward — and potentially quite costly — situation of having to change your company's name or the graphic appearance of the name.

The best way around that potential problem is to conduct a trademark search and, once you determine you are first on the scene, register the trademark with the U.S. Patent and Trademark Office (see address in box on page 73). A lawyer can advise you on conducting a proper search.

• *The broad application of copyrights.* Copyrights can apply not only to written material like books, brochures, and manuals but to paintings, music, photographs, and even computer software. Moreover, the protection is quite long — the life of the author plus fifty years for an individual and seventy-five to a hundred years for a company. A copyright doesn't need to be registered to be in effect.

■ Get the Protection You Need — and Can Afford

As you may have inferred from reading the previous section, the matter of legally protecting your intellectual property can get quite complex — and expensive. You likely don't want to spend endless hours sorting through legalisms with attorneys and paying huge fees to do so. On the other hand, you certainly don't want to leave yourself legally exposed or squander a competitive advantage because you didn't do what was legally necessary. So here are some tips for maximizing your protection at the lowest possible cost.

• *Patent only what is important.* Filing for a patent can be a tedious and time-consuming task if you are not properly prepared. Generally speaking, a patent lawyer needs background on the invention, information on exactly what you want to protect, and a list of the advantages of your invention. Ask the lawyer in advance what documentation you should gather together to support your claims. With proper preparation, it should be possible to complete much of the entrepreneur's work during a two-to-three hour conference with the lawyer.

Without legal complications, the process of filing a patent application in the United States will likely run $2,500 to $7,500 in legal fees; if you seek patents in major countries around the world, the legal fees can easily total $25,000 to $30,000 or more.

If there are challenges made by patent office examiners or competing individuals or companies, the American legal fees can soar. When new superconducting materials were discovered that could make possible the production of electricity without resistance, several companies filed patent applications covering the same formulations, and it was left to patent officials to sort things out. After the patent is awarded, there can be future court cases challenging the decision.

As a result, entrepreneurs are well advised to seek patent protection only when it is truly warranted. You must conclude, first, that you need the protection and, second, that you will recover much more than your expenditure in additional long-term sales.

• *Cover yourself internationally.* As I suggested in the previous point, you should be examining your patent possibilities not only in the United States, but overseas. With foreign competition as pervasive as it is, you must assume that what you want to protect in this country you will also want to protect in Europe and Asia.

While the patent application process has become more standardized in recent years, there are still important differences. One major difference between the U.S. procedure and that of many foreign countries involves application timing. The U.S. process recognizes the "first to invent," while the Japanese process recognizes the "first to file." Thus, in the United States, you must be able to document that you came up with the invention before others; in Japan you have to get to the patent office first. When there are possible competing claims for the same invention, as in the case of superconductivity noted earlier, such timing distinctions can be significant.

International considerations extend to trade secret and trademark protection as well. If there is any chance that you could sell your product or service overseas during the next few years, or if foreign competitors would be interested in selling your product overseas, by all means explore the options for international protection.

Generally speaking, you will keep your total costs down if you anticipate potential international considerations early so they can be dealt with together with domestic matters.

- **Get the best trademark protection as early as possible.** Some entrepreneurs assume that because they expect to only operate locally — say, have one store serving a single town or a service covering a particular county — they have all the protection they need when they incorporate with the state corporation office. Indeed, a business may operate for months or even years before a company in a neighboring town, county, or state with the same or similar name finds out about it — and sends a cease and desist letter. At that point, an entrepreneur faces two grim prospects: an expensive legal battle or changing the company's name or other aspects of its trademark.

Registering a trademark is a much simpler procedure than getting a patent. A trademark search can usually be done for a few hundred dollars; if there are potential conflicts discovered during the search, the legal costs can rise but if not the total process needn't exceed $1,000. And a change in the trademark laws in 1989 makes it possible to apply to register a trademark before you are using it.

- **Choose the right form of protection.** Don't assume that because copyright protection is cheaper to obtain than patent protection you should automatically go the less expensive route. It's widely assumed, for instance, that computer software can only be protected by copyright. In fact, it is possible to obtain patent protection for some software. The up-front cost for the patent will be greater than for the copyright, but it could turn out that the patent offers greater security from encroachment by competitors. The same applies to dress designs, new plant breeds, and a wide variety of other items. Spend the $200 or $300 it might cost to get sound legal answers to your questions.

- **Warn potential violators that you are serious.** Let individuals who become involved with your company know that its intellectual property is very important. This applies to new employees in

---

GOVERNMENT SOURCES OF PROTECTION

To file for a patent or register a trademark or service mark:

1. U.S. Patent and Trademark Office
   2021 Jefferson Davis Highway
   Arlington, VA 20231
   (703) 557-3158

For information on copyright protection and to register a copyright:

2. U.S. Copyright Office
   Library of Congress Bldg., Dept. DS
   Washington, DC 20402
   (202) 783-3238

particular as well as to suppliers and consultants. You should warn everyone who has access to important information that the nondisclosure and other agreements they sign are not just a formality. If someone does cross you up, be prepared to take legal action to set an example that will become known to others. Your readiness to back up your intellectual property rights will serve as a deterrent to those who try to take advantage of you.

• *Plan for information protection.* In the start-up phase, be prepared for the various disclosures of important information that you will need to make. This information may be contained in a business plan, lists of prospects, supplier names, production specifications, and various other data essential to starting your business.

As you begin to make contacts with potential investors, suppliers, and employees, be prepared with the right agreement, letter, or statement that each must sign. Obviously, you can't anticipate each need immediately, because some might develop as you build your business. But as much as possible, try to cover several contingencies simultaneously with lawyers to keep your costs down.

■ Concluding Note

Clearly, the matter of intellectual property is one that is growing in importance and complexity. From your viewpoint as an entrepreneur, the best approach is to view it as simply one more aspect of the management challenge. Just as you will need to manage people (discussed in the next chapter) and finances (discussed in Chapter 6), you will need to manage your intellectual property.

There's no reason why protecting your idea should limit your ability to build your business. If managed correctly, the process of protecting the idea and everything that goes with it should spell increased opportunity.

■ Exercise I: A Review

Fill in the blanks as required. The answers are provided at the bottom of the next page:

1. Your best protection against having your business idea stolen is to know the _____ of the person you discuss the idea with.

2. If you plan to write a _____ , be sure to _____ it and _____ the names of individuals who will receive a copy.

3. Ask those who will view your business plan to sign a _____- _____ _____ that prohibits their using or disclosing the information.

4. _____ limit the ability of someone who leaves your company from using proprietary materials, designs, and formulas or from taking customer names with them.

5. _____ may help prevent others from copying your invention.

6. _____ may help prevent others from copying the manual you plan to sell.

7. _____ may help prevent others from using a special logo you have designed for your business.

8. Employers should raise the _____ of litigation to potential employees to discourage them from stealing proprietary information.

9. While it's important to protect one's business interests, entrepreneurs should concentrate on the _____ of their companies.

10. Employers interested in protecting their rights should obtain the services of a qualified _____ .

■ Exercise II: An Intellectual Property Self-Assessment.

Listed below are eight common matters involving intellectual property. Next to each, write yes or no depending on whether it affects you. Also, provide a reason for your answer. If you are planning to open a dry-cleaning store, you may answer no for patents because you will be using machinery and processes already developed by others. But you may answer yes for trade secrets if you have access to a low-cost out-of-state supplier of cleaning chemicals that enables you to provide lower prices than your competitors. Or you may answer yes for copyright if you have put together a training manual for new employees.

    If you are uncertain about your answers to any of the items, be sure to consult with a lawyer with expertise in intellectual property matters.

• **Copyright**

• **Employment agreement**

• **Noncompete agreement**

• **Nondisclosure agreement**

• **Patent**

• **Service mark**

• **Trademark**

• **Trade secret**

ANSWERS TO EXERCISE I		
1. Character	5. Patents	8. Threat
2. Business plan, number, record	6. Copyrights	9. Growth
3. Nondisclosure agreement	7. Trademarks	10. Attorney
4. Employee agreements	or Servicemarks	

CHAPTER FOUR

THE RIGHT PEOPLE

*"People are the agony
and the ecstasy of my company."*
....
Donald Burr, founder of People Express

You hear it over and over: a business is only as good as its people.

Frank Carney of Pizza Hut expresses the point well: "Your employees are your only link with your customers. It is very important when you first open to show your customers you care and provide for them in terms of the experiences they have. You do that with good people, because whether customers are coming back will be based on the quality of their experiences. In the quality you can have great food and give somebody bad service. . . .You really have to get people who understand customers as guests, and guests need to be treated just like a guest in your home."

The people issue promises to become more critical during the 1990s. That's because consumers' expectations about the quality of the products and services they buy keep increasing. Simultaneously, the pool of qualified employees appears to be getting smaller, due in part to demographics and our nation's educational system. After the baby boom ended in 1964, the birth rate declined sharply, and population growth has continued to slow since then.

The slowdown in population growth coincided with a

deterioration in the nation's educational system. By some estimates, as many as one in five workers was functionally illiterate
in the early 1990's. Essentially, there are fewer properly educated
young people entering the work force to serve an ever-more
demanding marketplace.

The Small Business Administration, in a report projecting
major challenges of the 1990s, points out that "small businesses
may find it more difficult to recruit a work force like that which
they have employed in the past. . . . The changing composition of
the labor force will affect productivity, the demand for benefits vis-
a-vis wages, the relative rigidity or flexibility of the work force, and
the flexibility of small businesses."

One effect of these trends is intensified competition for the best
people. Major corporations are as intent on finding top employees
as are start-up businesses. In some cases, the large corporations
have initiated education and training programs to teach employees
everything from reading to advanced math to computer skills.

■ The Start-up Company's Dilemma

Chances are, you're beginning to feel a bit uncomfortable with
what I've said, and for good reason. Here I am concluding that you're
supposed to go head-to-head with the biggest corporations in the
country for the best employees, and you don't even have enough
money to pay rent or buy adequate supplies. How are you going to pay
the salaries, let alone provide the fancy benefit programs, that large
corporations provide?

Indeed, this is the start-up company's major dilemma. There's no
question that success in your business requires that you have the best
people possible. But it also requires that you be able to pay them.

I should point out that the dilemma never truly ends. The
problem of finding and keeping the best people is one of the most
daunting that entrepreneurs face. If you ask a business owner about
his or her most difficult challenge, he or she will invariably point to

"the people problem."

Somehow it seems as if from employees' viewpoints, the business owner is never quite paying enough. And from the owner's vantage point, it appears that people aren't working as hard or as smart as they should be.

■ The Clash of Philosophies

One thing that becomes clear as you listen to successful entrepreneurs describe their experiences trying to find and motivate the best people is that they tend to have strong viewpoints or philosophies about the people issue. Consider the opposing viewpoints of Frank Carney of Pizza Hut and Gordon Segal of Crate & Barrel about the kind of people you should initially seek out.

Here is Carney's philosophy: "For a business to be successful, you have to have a lot of different skills, and it is good to find somebody not exactly like you, somebody who has complementary skills. If you are a marketing-oriented or a people-oriented person, you need somebody who is a control and accounting person to give you the balance you need."

Gordon Segal takes this view: "I think that in hiring your first people what is important is that they have to be much like you. I think you have to understand that they go out in the marketplace and they represent you in the store — they are you. So their personality has to be one that you can really trust. . . . If you are extroverted and positive and enthusiastic, you can't hire somebody who is introverted, negative, and hates people. It just doesn't work. You have to get the same kind of personality that you are."

While Carney advises you to find others who complement your skills and experience, Segal suggests you try to find more people with your own attributes, since it is your positive outlook and commitment that will likely determine success or failure. I believe it is safe to say that a new business should be seeking to do both — find people who bring new skills to the business and others who have the founder's enthusiasm and optimistic outlook.

Such divergences in opinions occur on other issues as well. Some entrepreneurs feel it is important to make stock available to motivate employees, while others are dead set against providing it. Some feel that having one or more partners is a way to improve the chances of a venture's success, while others are so against the partnership option that they can't discuss the idea rationally.

What is going on here? Behind such differences in philosophy are differences in experiences. Carney did quite well by using his approach of bringing in people with strengths different from his own, while Segal has been very successful relying on people with his own attributes.

Similarly, some entrepreneurs in partnerships have seen their businesses grow and prosper. Others have seen businesses that they felt should have been successful torn asunder by partnerships that didn't work — and they have sworn off partnerships forever.

So as I review different aspects of the people issue, keep in mind that one size does not fit all. What works for one entrepreneur may or may not work for you. As much as possible, I identify the circumstances under which various techniques work best.

■ Getting a Grip on the Problem

Clearly, then there's no simple answer to the dilemma surrounding that of people. But there are a variety of potential solutions. Part of the solution is to realize that finding the right people isn't a single major problem but a combination of several smaller problems.

Once you begin to pinpoint these individual problems, you find that each has a variety of potential solutions. It is important to realize that the people problem isn't simply a matter of hiring employees. The people issue extends beyond that to such other issues as involving business partners, bringing in service professionals, recruiting directors, and using outside contractors. You may conclude that bringing a partner in at the very beginning is preferable to trying to find money to hire an employee. Or you may decide on the opposite approach.

Each area poses its own set of challenges. In the area of employees, you may find yourself struggling with the notion of how to pay an initial full-time salesperson. Yet it may be possible to find an individual willing to work part-time on a commission-only basis, meaning that the person doesn't get paid until he or she makes a sale. It may also be possible to work with a manufacturer's rep or via some other distributor arrangement to avoid hiring your own salespeople.

In the area of service professionals, you may conclude that you need some expensive consulting help that you can't afford. However, rather than doing without, you may want to assemble an advisory board of experienced entrepreneurs or make use of a government-sponsored consulting service that is free to small companies.

The rest of this chapter examines these and other people issues.

■ Your First Employees

When a company first starts out, the founder often does everything, from testing the idea to writing the business plan to selling the product or service to sending out bills to taking out the garbage. But at some point early in the life of the business, the founder discovers that he or she can't do everything and hope to remain sane or grow the business. A business that is going to expand must somehow involve other people to handle the increasing number and complexity of tasks.

For a manufacturing business, those tasks may involve running machinery and assembling products. For a retail business, the tasks may include waiting on customers and locating additional inventory. For a service business, the tasks may be to complete a client engagement and produce marketing materials.

Whatever the business and the tasks at hand, hiring the first employees is perhaps the most intimidating step most entrepreneurs face. After all, hiring a new employee has all kinds of ramifications beyond the actual choice of the person.

Bringing employees on board means making a huge commitment. They are depending on your company for their very livelihood.

Because there are few hard-and-fast rules, I have tried to deal with the most common issues about hiring that first employee in a question-answer format.

I definitely need some help in my business, but I am not sure I need or can afford a full-time employee. Are there any other options available to me?

There are at least two other options and all start-up entrepreneurs should consider them seriously before hiring a full-time employee. One option is to bring on a contract employee. This is really a person you use almost as a consultant — typically on an hourly basis or on a task basis. You may arrange for the person to put in ten hours a week, or you may pay a flat fee for the person to accomplish a specific job that needs completing each month, such as delivering your food product to stores or calling customers who are late in paying their bills.

Contract employees have two main advantages: first, you don't have to worry about providing them with benefits like health and life insurance. Second, you can terminate them on short notice without feeling much guilt, since that is the nature of the relationship. (For an important disadvantage, see the box on page 83.)

Another option to avoid hiring a full-time employee is to hire a part-time. The person might work for your company twenty or thirty hours a week at a regular salary. The main advantage is that you get some help but at a lower total outlay than with a full-time person. Part-time employees often don't expect the same health and other benefits, which can further lower your total expenses.

What qualities should I look for in my first employees?

There's nearly unanimous agreement among entrepreneurs to seek the very best people possible. This is particularly important for a start-up company, because the first people hired inevitably bear a tremendous amount of responsibility as not only the front line but the only line.

Frank Carney expresses it this way: "You either have to hire smart or manage hard. You really have to pay attention if you are hiring in the key positions in your company. You need to take a lot of time and make sure you got the right person. . . . When you first start a business, you are after people who are going to be with you for some time. They are going to be essential to your success."

Mo Siegel's approach to hiring people is as follows: "I believe you should surround yourself with the best possible people you can. One of the things I did from the very beginning was that two or three or four years in advance, I would bring people into the company who were much more qualified than me and who had run much bigger businesses than the size of our business. Their strength was that they could see our business very clearly — they could see how to move it very clearly,

THE CONTRACT EMPLOYEE TRAP

To avoid having to hire full-time employees early on, some entrepreneurs rely on so-called contract employees. These are individuals hired on an hourly basis as needed. They are usually paid an hourly rate higher than they would earn if they were employed full-time, but they don't get benefits and are used only as needed to keep overhead down.

Be careful about using contract employees, however. The Internal Revenue Service has cracked down on using contract employees, sometimes redesignating them as regular employees.

The designation becomes very important for tax purposes. If an employee is considered a regular employee, the company is responsible for paying withholding and Social Security taxes. A change in designation can make a young company responsible for hundreds or even thousands of dollars of back taxes.

It's not a pleasant situation for a start-up company facing dozens of other problems. The main prevention: discuss the matter with an accountant.

and they were impatient with themselves to be running something bigger than something smaller. So they wanted to move it at a good pace to make it bigger."

How can I identify the best people?

Most entrepreneurs I know feel that the best people are those who have a track record of success at other organizations. The candidates you find through newspaper want ads often don't meet the qualifications you are looking for or have not been successful elsewhere.

Mo Siegel's approach illustrates this idea: "I hire winning players from winning teams because I found out a long time ago that if I hire a winning player from a losing team, the winning player from the losing team has learned how to justify failure. A winning player from a winning team learns to live with success and expects a lot more of it."

Christine Martindale of Esprit Miami has a similar attitude. "I hire employees on a gut feeling. . . . When I go against my feeling about someone and I hire under a desperate circumstance — if I say to myself, this is better than nothing — it never turns out right. You have to be willing to work through a lack of employees in order to get the right one, because if you don't get the right one, you are just going to have to replace that person in another six months."

How can I attract the best people when I can't afford to match the salaries they've been making elsewhere?

Most successful entrepreneurs will tell you that it's possible to attract top people other than with cash. One thing that attracts people is the possibility of being involved in an exciting venture that they can contribute to.

According to Gordon Segal, "You attract a good person by having a great idea, a wonderful environment, treating him or her with dignity and respect, and providing a lot of responsibility.

I think this is very basic. You have to have a belief in a company. I believe that there is a belief and a philosophy that you can deliver and get these people who work with you to believe in these beliefs. Then the company has a mission, and consequently, people can work toward this goal and feel good about it."

George Kachajian of Silicon Technology seconds that notion. "When you have nothing, you have to put yourself in their place and you try to get them to share your dream of what your business is all about. That requires a lot of communication and a lot of openness, a lot of meetings and discussions, and you don't hold anything back. You just lay it all out for them to see the business the same way you do. And generate the same kind of commitment that you have. If you can do that, you are a good manager."

But, of course, enthusiasm, dignity, and respect can go only so far. There must be financial compensation.

For start-up companies, which tend to be short on cash, there is usually one form of compensation in abundant supply: equity. Company stock can indeed be an important commodity for those entrepreneurs who can convince potential employees that the company will succeed, thus making the equity much more valuable in the future.

Christine Martindale used this technique to lure one of her earliest employees. "When I started in business, the girl who came to work for me as a secretary took a $200-a-month pay cut from her previous job and I gave her 5% of the company. I promised her within a year that I would pay her $200 more than she was making at her other job."

But if I make stock available, don't I run the risk of losing control of the company or having disgruntled shareholders from among employees who leave some time in the future?

This is a common concern among start-up entrepreneurs. If you don't have enough cash and don't want to make stock available to attract the best people, you must seriously con–

TANGIBLE VS. INTANGIBLE BENEFITS

Entrepreneurs often fret that their start-up company can't afford to provide its first employees with such benefits as health and disability insurance.

It's important to keep in mind that not all benefits have to be expensive. Many start-up companies are capable of offering important benefits to employees that, at first glance, might not even seem significant enough to be categorized as benefits.

Consider a flexible schedule that allows a mother of young children to report for work any time between 7:00 a.m. and 10:00 a.m. and leave eight hours after reporting. Providing the mother an opportunity to get her children ready for school some days and have a baby-sitter come early on other days, may be more important than any insurance you could provide.

Or consider having a lunch room with a microwave oven and a small refrigerator. By making it easier for employees to bring their lunches and save the $15 or $20 weekly that it costs to eat out, you may have a very popular benefit.

Such so-called intangible benefits are often more important to employees than the traditional tangible ones. Intangible benefits can include discounts on company merchandise, access to the company truck on weekends, and company picnics or other outings. They are limited only by your imagination.

sider devising other incentives for your first employees. Perhaps you can provide a bonus or commission plan instead of giving up stock.

But, as Mo Siegel points out, the fear about making stock available is often irrational when examined in a larger perspective. "If you don't have money and you want to lure someone into your organization who is really critical to its growth and development, figure out a stock deal. If you could get someone in who could make your company two or three times its size, but you have to give up some percent — say, 5% of your company or 2% or whatever — give the person the 2% and double the company, give 5% and double. Who cares? Look at what you are going to get."

Just a note of caution at this point: consult with an attorney or accountant to determine the best way to structure any such arrangements. You'll need to come up with a fair valuation of the company's stock. It's likely you'll not want to make all the stock available at once, but over a period of three to five years, so that as an employee proves him or herself, the stock becomes available. And you'll want to have a buy-back provision that gives you the right of first refusal should a former employee want to get rid of stock. Otherwise, you could find yourself an unwanted stranger as a shareholder in your company.

My tendency is to do everything myself because employees aren't as committed as I am. What can I do to gain the necessary commitment besides encourage them and give them money and stock?

There is no way to ensure that your employees will ever be quite as committed as you are, even if you make available small amounts of stock. One key to gaining commitment is to give employees responsibility and authority — that is, delegate.

"You have to learn how to delegate," says David Liederman. "Most entrepreneurs want to do everything themselves, and they get into trouble. There are some people in this life who know how to do things better than you do."

Delegating successfully requires that you explain to employees exactly what is expected of them and on what timetable, and then give them the leeway to accomplish the task in the best way they know how. Most people want to do a good job, but they need the right conditions to perform properly. These conditions can include training or tools or the absence of burdensome rules. Some people do best with someone looking over their shoulders, but most do best when given some latitude. If properly encouraged, employees will often surprise you with their ingenuity.

■ Partnership: A Business Marriage

Business partnerships are among the most emotional situations confronting entrepreneurs. I've heard more than one entrepreneur compare partnership with marriage. As in marriage, a business partnership often can't stand up to the intense demands of open communication and fluctuating fortunes, and the equivalent of a divorce often results.

As is true in marriage, it's a lot easier to get into a partnership than to get out of it. Even in family businesses, brother can be pitted against brother in agonizing confrontation.

An accountant I know who specializes in working with small businesses recounts the tale of two brothers who started a manufacturing business from scratch and over twelve years built it to $15 million in annual sales. While the two seemed to get along fine to outsiders, there were serious tensions below the surface. One morning the older brother walked into work and found a note from his younger sibling that read: "Can no longer live with our relationship. We have to break up. Let's bid against each other to decide who gets to keep the business. Highest bidder wins."

Needless to say, the older brother was shocked. He was about to call his accountant and attorney but stopped. The two brothers used the same professionals, and the older brother wondered if his sibling had already been in touch with them — and whether they had taken sides. He wondered the same thing about friends and relatives.

Many months of negotiations followed. Would the brothers simply split up the business? Would one brother buy out the other? What would the purchase price be? Would a noncompete agreement be necessary to prevent the brother who sold out from starting a similar business?

Eventually, the brothers worked out an accommodation. But not without much heartache and damage to the business, as sales declined while they were absorbed with their negotiations. While these brothers wound up on speaking terms, in some cases that is not true.

Business partnerships sometimes lead to many years of family divisiveness and bitterness.

Even when a partnership succeeds, many note, it is not without its ups and downs. Because the demands of starting a business are so intense in and of themselves, a partnership relationship adds another layer of complexity.

A number of the entrepreneurs I interviewed had been through unhappy partnerships, and the scars are very much evident as they tell their stories.

David Liederman says he had two unsuccessful partnerships before starting David's Cookies by himself. He wound up "in litigation against them. I wouldn't do it again with partners."

Christine Martindale recalls that before she started Esprit Miami, she was involved in another business. "My other business was also the same type of operation. The woman that I spoke about that encouraged me to go into business was my partner and we had another partner and it was thirds. I was advised from the beginning not to go thirds because two gang up on the other at some point in time. After a year the two partners and I had a disagreement, and I was the only one working in the company, so I quit and they went out of business. But they tried to control me, control what I was doing, by voting against me together. So when I started the second company, I had 75% and I still maintain control, even though I have taken on additional partners and I won't give up control."

■ Is a Partnership for You?

There is no one right answer to this question. The right answer for you depends partly on the needs of your business and your ability to handle the demands of partnership.

One approach to assessing the answer for yourself can be gleaned from the self-evaluation James Lowry went through before starting his consulting firm:

"When I started my business I, like many others, thought about forming a partnership. . . and I approached several people. But as I reflected on it, [I concluded] it was basically out of fear. I said that I can't do it myself, so if I have two or three other people to lean on, it might be easier. And I think 90% of the bad mistakes of partnerships are made because of that same reason. People don't feel that they can do it by themselves, and they enter into contracts with people who are usually very good friends, close relationships but bad partners. A partnership in business is like a partnership in marriage. Unless you are compatible, unless you can work together, unless you can argue, unless you can fight, unless you can commiserate and do all those things that a good partner in marriage can do, it is going to fail."

It's possible to interpret Lowry as saying that anyone who starts a business with partners is doing it out of insecurity. I don't believe that is his intention. His real message is that if you are considering a business partnership, think long and hard about whether it makes sense for *you* before making any final commitments.

After all, there are situations in which a partnership makes sense. For example, many high-technology firms require an assortment of technical, marketing, and financial skills very early on, and these are best handled by a team of people that can be most easily assembled through a partnership.

As in marriage, there are no ways to guarantee the success of a business partnership. You can only take steps to improve your chances of success. Here are some suggestions for doing that:

• *Know what you want from a partner.*

James Lowry articulated this point well. You need to determine whether you really need and want a partner. Do you want the partner to invest money? Are you looking for a particular skill or set of skills, such as experience setting up a production line? Do you need to get that skill in a partner, or could you obtain those skills by hiring someone? Do you want a partner to help relieve the loneliness and uncertainty that are part and parcel of starting a company?

There's nothing wrong with wanting a partner for his or her financial assistance or to help relieve the loneliness. What is important is that you identify your needs so you can better determine if a partner is the answer to those needs.

• **Be very selective in your choice of partners.**

Not only should you know your potential partner very well, but you should also know each other in a business environment. Ideally, you will have worked together and thus recognize each other's professional strengths and weaknesses.

Being good friends on a social level isn't enough. If you are considering a partnership with a friend, try to get input from people who have worked with the friend — almost in the manner of an employment reference.

The same applies to relatives. You may think you know your brother-in-law well, but being in business together will quickly expose personal and managerial weaknesses.

Any potential partner will have both strengths and weaknesses. Determine beforehand whether the strengths outweigh the weaknesses to warrant a productive relationship.

• **Don't fall into the trap of automatically dividing ownership up evenly.**

Just because three people are going into business together doesn't mean that each partner should own one-third of the business. If one of the partners has already negotiated some contracts or sales that will bring in cash from the start, that partner may be entitled to a larger share of the company. Or it may be that one partner will start out working full-time while two others work part-time until the business grows. A strong argument can be made for the full-time person getting a larger piece of the business in consideration of the larger risk he or she is taking by making an initial full-time commitment.

Christine Martindale took a larger chunk of equity when she began Esprit Miami after her unhappy partnership experience.

She adds: "Partnership gave me security. One partner was a wholesaler in the business. I called him every day. He gave me advice and he encouraged me. He kept me going when I lost money. He would say that everyone loses money. You just don't want to do it again. If I received a bad shipment, he would say you have to expect those things sometimes. Just order some more. He kept me going. My second group of partners have been extremely supportive. I am glad now that I have partners."

- **Negotiate a written agreement covering key partnership issues.**

As was noted at the outset of this section, a business partnership is much like marriage. If a partner dies, is disabled, or wants a "divorce," the situation can become very messy legally. A written agreement can head off a thorny legal predicament by providing specific procedures for various scenarios.

One of the most common scenarios is that a partner leaves the business — perhaps for personal reasons or even because of death. There need to be provisions covering the sale of that partner's shares in the company. Does the company have right of first refusal on the stock? How will the stock price be established? Can the company pay the partner off over a period of years?

Christine Martindale recalls dealing with this situation: "I went to a lawyer and got a buy/sell agreement because in a privately held corporation, if you don't have a buy/sell agreement, then your rights aren't protected. Your partner could go out and sell his interest in the company to anyone that he wanted, and that person would have the right to interfere in the way that you operate. You have to both say what you expect of each other. I expect you to give me $10,000, and you expect me to pay back in five years. It has to be very clear."

Notice that Martindale says that she went to a lawyer. Two or three partners can agree on a single attorney to work out the agreement for them, or each partner can have his or her own personal attorney providing advice on appropriate terms. It depends on how well the partners know each other, how the attorneys feel, and how complex the situation is. The more complex the situation, the more likely it is that you will want an attorney of your own to review whatever is worked out among the partners to make sure that your personal interests are properly tended to.

• *Hope for the best and anticipate the worst.*
Martindale sums up the typical partnership relationship when she observes: "It doesn't matter [what agreement you have] as long as the money is good. As long as the money is coming in fine and everyone is happy and the business is doing well, it doesn't matter. But as soon as the partners start losing money or the business is having problems, like if it gets in trouble with the IRS, then people start fighting. That's when partnerships break up and that's when companies go under."

■ Make Use of Skilled Professionals

At an annual *Inc.* Conference on Growing the Company, Peter Ueberroth, the organizer of the 1984 Olympics and former major league baseball commissioner, gave a keynote address in which he warned the 800-plus small-company executives about the importance of their service professionals. "You will need to learn to demand service," he advised. "Of whom? Of your lawyers, accountants, and consultants. You can't just have an accountant. You'd better get a damned good one. In my experience, 20% are good to great, 50% are mediocre, and 30% are bad. You'd better be dealing with that 20%. Rethink your lawyers and accountants. They should not just be a neighbor you play golf with. They'd better win for you."

According to the successful entrepreneurs interviewed, a good service professional can save a lot of headaches. When asked what she might do differently if she were starting a business again, Christine Martindale answered: "I think I would have hired an accountant. . . .

I had no idea what my expenses were. I didn't know how to report to my growers. I didn't know how to pay my bills. All I knew was how to sell, and that's what I would do. I think that you hire a professional bookkeeper, a professional accountant, not an independent accountant. I would go with one of the big firms. They have small-business departments and they lease out those people who are also rookies, but you have the experience of all the senior partners behind them. Get a good accountant and a good bookkeeper."

That's easy for her to say, you're probably thinking, but suppose you can't afford to pay the high hourly rates many accountants and attorneys charge? James Lowry suggests you try to be creative about possible arrangements:

"There is no question that accountants, legal advisers, and lawyers cost money. They really do cost money. And they are working on hourly rates, just like you are. But I think you have to approach them, just like I approached them, and say, 'Look, I am a small guy now, but I am going to grow. I am going to pay you for your services. It won't be as much as you demand with somebody else, but I am going to pay you. But believe me, as I grow, I will never leave you as long as you provide good levels of quality service. I will never leave you. We are in this fight together.' I told that to my lawyer, my accountant, and my tax adviser, and they are all with me now eleven years later."

◼ A Board of Advisers

As the previous section makes clear, entrepreneurs need all the advice they can get when starting out, but often they can't afford to pay for it. Negotiating lower rates with service professionals is one possible way to cut down the costs. Another is to assemble a board of advisers or outside board of directors — a group of three to seven business experts — to act as a sounding board about major decisions and challenges confronting the new business.

A board of advisers has become increasingly preferred by both entrepreneurs and potential advisers because of legal problems that crop up for outside directors. A board of directors in a corporation has the legal power to make important decisions, such as who the senior officers are or whether the company should make acquisitions or be put up for sale (described in greater detail in the next chapter).

In addition, directors have become more frequent targets of legal action by disgruntled shareholders, who accuse the directors of failing to protect the shareholders' interests. Thus, outside directors have had to concern themselves with protecting their legal exposure when serving as outside directors.

These problems have discouraged both entrepreneurs and potential outside directors from involving themselves with the process and made the concept of a nonlegal board of advisers preferable. The board of advisers typically is formed in addition to a board of directors, which consists of the company's founders and possibly such senior advisers as the company's attorney or accountant.

One advantage of an advisory board over service professionals is that the board's advice is often more frank and impartial because the advisers aren't dependent on the company for earning a living. Here are some tips on assembling an advisory board:

- **Seek out knowledgeable and experienced business experts.**

  Typically, these will be successful entrepreneurs in related but noncompeting businesses or business school professors. Ideally, they will have experience working with start-up companies, so they can be sensitive to the special challenges that confront your company.

- **Focus on strategic issues.**

  Try not to burden your advisory board with petty issues, such as what kind of copier to buy or terms of your office lease. Instead, attempt to deal with such matters as identifying emerging market segments and ways to motivate your sales force.

  To reinforce your businesslike approach, schedule monthly or bimonthly meetings and have an agenda prepared in advance.

• *Try to reward your board.*

Ideally, you should pay the members of your advisory board a regular meeting fee of $500 or $1,000. In the early stages of your business, when there's little cash flow, members will understand if you can't compensate them in cash. But even in that circumstance, try to come up with other ways to show your appreciation. Have dinner meetings at a restaurant where you pick up the tab or take everyone to a ball game.

■ Exercise 1: Personal Assessment

A. In the four columns below, list your business-related strengths and weaknesses, likes and dislikes. Include personal traits, skills, and behavior. For example, if you like numbers but dislike making presentations to groups of people, write that down. If you don't enjoy working with raw data or performing in-depth analysis but would rather spend your time in people-oriented situations, then put that down.

This exercise will better enable you to determine the personal contributions you will bring to your own company as well as define the gaps that can be filled by hiring qualified key employees. I have provided a short Sample Table followed by one you can use for your own assessment.

Sample Table

Strengths	Weaknesses	Likes	Dislikes
Investing	Marketing	Analysis	Selling
Hiring	Advertising	Bookkeeping	Planning

Now, choose from the traits in the Sample Table or add some of your own:

Strengths	Weaknesses	Likes	Dislikes

B. Now you should have some specific ideas about the qualities you'd most like to see in your employees. Next, think about the skills, traits, and background you would like to see your key employees possess. Prioritize them from the most to the least important.

1.

2.

3.

4.

C. Based on the qualities you have prioritized, write a brief job description (no more than seventy-five words) for each of the key people you plan to hire.

■ Exercise II: Salaries

Briefly answer the following questions in one or two sentences:

1. **What is the market value for each individual described in the previous section?**
   a.
   b.
   c.
   d.

2. **What salary might he or she expect to receive from one of your competitors?**
   a.
   b.
   c.
   d.

3. What salary are you prepared to offer?

    a.

    b.

    c.

    d.

4. Are there other forms of compensation or benefits that you might provide in lieu of extra money?

5. When do you need to bring these people on board? Write a schedule of when you plan to have each person working for your company.

    a.

    b.

    c.

    d.

6. Where do you plan to find these people (want ads, contacts, competing companies, etc.)? List at least four potential sources of candidates.

    a.

    b.

    c.

    d.

7. Aside from the financial/benefits package you will offer, how do you plan to sell the candidates on your company? Provide three reasons why prospective employees should take a chance with your start-up company.

    a.

    b.

    c.

■ Exercise III: Outside Advisers

A. List by name prospective outsiders who can contribute to your operation by providing valuable advice and services.

- **Bookkeeper**

- **Accountant**

- **Attorney**

- **Consultant**

B. List five candidates for an outside board of advisers or as outside directors for your company.

1.

2.

3.

4.

5.

STRUCTURING THE BUSINESS

*"The most important consideration you
can have in running a business is to stay legal."*

George Kachajian, Silicon Technology Inc.

As you go through the process of starting a business, at some point you'll have to confront the issue of its structure. A good time is after you've tested the idea and have begun to think about bringing other people on board.

I'll be the first to agree that this isn't the most exciting part of starting a business. In many respects, it's downright boring having to focus on legal and tax issues, which are the driving forces behind the structure you choose.

You'll quickly notice that this chapter has less of the "I was there" flavor provided by the successful entrepreneurs in the previous chapters. There's a reason for that. Entrepreneurs tend to view the organizational issues as mechanistic and legalistic — outside their sphere of interests and expertise and thus best left to attorneys.

But as anyone starting out in business quickly discovers, legal and tax issues are the stuff of which significant dollars are often made. If you structure your business inappropriately, you could be subject to costly legal expenses when you try to correct the problem later. You could also wind up paying many thousands of dollars more in taxes than you should.

Moreover, the legal and tax issues can have a ripple effect on other aspects of the start-up process. For instance, whether you organize as a partnership or a corporation could affect your ability to obtain a bank loan or investment funds. It could affect your ability to use stock as an incentive to attract new employees. It could also affect the type and cost of benefit programs you can offer. And, as George Kachajian of Silicon Technology suggests in his quote at the beginning of this chapter, being on the up-and-up legally helps set the tone for the entire business. To be successful, honesty is essential in your dealings with customers, suppliers, lenders, employees, and the many others your business comes into contact with. There's no better place to begin your efforts to be legally correct than in structuring your business.

Fortunately, the matter of structuring your business isn't all that complicated. Basically, you have three choices: a sole proprietorship, a partnership, or a corporation. Each choice has its pros and its cons, which I address. The choices also vary somewhat in complexity. A sole proprietorship is usually the simplest structure, while a partnership and corporation can vary widely in their complexity.

Nor is the matter of a business's structure an all-or-none decision. It's possible to begin as a sole proprietorship and later turn the business into a partnership or a corporation — or vice versa. This doesn't mean the decision on structure should be made casually, however. While changes can be made, the larger and more mature the business becomes, the more complex changes in structure become.

■ A Sole Proprietorship

In a sole proprietorship, a business and its owner are essentially one and the same. Sole proprietorships are generally service businesses that can be handled by one person, such as a plumbing, copywriting, or consulting business. While sole proprietorships tend to be limited to one person, they can hire employees.

Sole proprietorships comprise the bulk of all businesses; approximately 70% of the nation's more than 20 million businesses consist of sole proprietorships. Of course, in many cases these sole proprietorships are part-time businesses established as much for tax write-off purposes as for their money-earning potential.

The Advantages

The main advantage of a sole proprietorship is its simplicity to establish and operate. Because there's no need for a company charter or special papers, you don't need an attorney's help to set it up.

Taxes are similarly straightforward. You report your business income and expenses on Schedule C of your personal income tax return. Your profit or loss is then combined with your other income.

The inclusion of your business income on your personal taxes can lead to lower tax rates than if your business were incorporated, because personal rates tend to be lower than corporate rates and you avoid local corporate taxes required by many states.

The Disadvantages

The main disadvantage of being a sole proprietorship is a potential legal one. Because you and the business are one and the same, you are personally liable for its debts and other problems that may arise.

Therefore, if the business runs into financial problems, creditors can come after your personal assets, including your house, to obtain payment. Similarly, if your business injures someone or otherwise harms that person so that they sue you, any financial obligations that result and aren't covered by insurance can be yours personally.

If a sole proprietorship begins to grow and hire employees, the potential legal problems only multiply. If an employee is injured working for you or causes injury to a customer, as the owner you could be personally responsible, depending on the situation.

Sole proprietorships also tend to find financing difficult to come by, either for start up or expansion. Banks and professional investors prefer the legal protection afforded by a corporation and thus tend to avoid sole proprietorships.

The tax benefits of not having to pay corporate taxes can be at least partially outweighed by the fact that you can't deduct all your payments for health insurance and other benefits you may pro–vide yourself.

Getting Started

While the federal government has no special requirements for es-tablishing a sole proprietorship, state and local governments often do. You may need to obtain certain local licenses. If you are preparing food products, for instance, you may need a license from the local board of health. If you are an employment or education counselor, you may need to fulfill certification requirements to receive a license and open a practice.

If your business will be started out of your home, you may have to register with county or town officials. This can lead you into the tricky area of zoning regulations, which determine how neighbor-hoods and buildings can be used. For example, some localities allow businesses to be operated from the home, provided no signs are posted. So if you plan to name your business something other than your name, you wouldn't be able to hang a sign outside. But if the business is Smith Associates, you can at least hang a sign outside that says Smith.

Another matter that needs tending to is that of insurance. You should insure any equipment against damage or theft. You should also have liability insurance to protect you if someone is injured using your product or while doing business on your property. In certain professions, it may be advisable to have specialized liability insur-ance, such as medical malpractice insurance for doctors and libel insurance for writers. Other insurance areas to investigate are coverage for medical care if someone is injured while visiting your business and for lost business in the event a fire or storm shuts your business down for an extended period.

Clearly, a good insurance agent can help steer you toward the types and amounts of coverage that best suit your needs and your budget.

■ Partnership

I discussed the matter of partners to some extent in the previous chapter but more in the generic sense. It's possible, for instance, for two or three people to form a business together and incorporate it. Thus, while they are working as partners, they do not have a partnership in a legal or tax sense.

Two or more people may also establish a partnership for legal and tax purposes. A partnership agreement should be drawn up to define the rights and obligations of each partner. Such a partnership files a tax return that computes partnership income and loss. Each partner's share of the income or loss, however, is reported on his or her personal tax return.

The Advantages

A partnership allows a group of owners to get tax benefits similar to those of a sole proprietorship. As noted earlier, individual tax rates tend to be lower than corporate rates.

A partnership also allows for much flexibility in distribution of ownership and income. It may be that there are senior partners who get a larger stake in the business and share of profits than junior partners. Or it could be that income is tied to the amount of business each partner brings in.

The flexibility also allows new partners to be added over time as they prove their ability to contribute to the business. Partnership income in this situation is constantly being redistributed.

The possibility of becoming a partner in a thriving business becomes an important incentive to new employees. The flexibility and motivational aspects of the partnership arrangement have been exploited most effectively by professional service firms — principally law and accounting firms.

The Disadvantages

The main drawbacks of a partnership are the same as those associated with a sole proprietorship. The partners are each personally liable for any debts if the business fails or insurance fails to cover obligations from an accident or lawsuit. In addition, bankers and investors are usually reluctant to make funds available to a partnership because of the potential legal complications that can result.

A partnership can also be subject to serious tensions if the business situation goes less favorably than the partners anticipated. As described in the previous chapter, these interpersonal tensions can be quite intense. But they can carry over to the legal aspect of the partnership as well.

Even assuming the partnership has a well-conceived written agreement, there can be disputes if one partner wants to leave the business or several partners want one partner to leave. These disputes may be over the value of the departing partner's share in the business or the timing of those payments.

What to Do

A key to a successful legal partnership is the quality of the written agreement that sets out the partnership's terms. The more clearly and realistically this agreement anticipates possible future occurrences, the more likely the partnership will be able to weather adversity.

One of the most important sections of any partnership agreement is the buy-sell agreement. This provides terms covering the departure of one or more partners from death, disability, retirement, or resignation. A partnership will usually want to carry life insurance on each partner so that if one partner dies, the partnership will be able to pay that partner's estate for the value of his or her interest in the business.

Other eventualities, though, are less clear cut and need to be negotiated. There should be a way to value the business if one partner resigns and wants to sell his or her interest. There also needs to be a way to set the length of the payout terms so that the business isn't burdened with suddenly having to make such a huge payment to one partner that the business's viability is jeopardized.

It certainly simplifies the process if a single attorney prepares the partnership agreement and is available to advise the business as it implements the agreement. But each partner should still have his or her own personal attorney review the agreement to make sure each partner's individual interests are protected.

As noted earlier in this section, partnership agreements seem to work best for professional service firms. They don't work as well for companies that make products because of the personal legal exposure for each partner and the need for financing that usually arises as the company expands.

■ Incorporation

If you expect your business to have employees or obtain financing soon after starting up, you will probably want to be incorporated. Otherwise, you can begin as a sole proprietorship or partnership with the intention to change over to a corporate structure when the time is right.

Technically, the process of incorporating is fairly straightforward. You fill out some forms, provide documentation about who the shareholders and officers are, and pay a state fee of $500 to $1,000.

You will want the assistance of an attorney, though, to help in setting up the corporate rules covering the election of directors, the company's capital structure, and advice on where to incorporate. You will probably want to incorporate in the state that will be the company's home base. But in some circumstances you may be better off incorporating in another state — usually Delaware — because of more flexible rules governing corporations as well as tax benefits. The downside of the out-of-state incorporation is that there may be additional taxes or penalties in your home state.

Another choice you will confront is whether to organize as a C corporation or an S corporation. A C corporation allows maximum flexibility — with no limitations on the number of shareholders or classes of stock. It pays separate corporate taxes.

An S corporation is meant to help small companies gain a corporate structure without being penalized on the tax front. Its main attraction is that profits and losses flow directly to the company's shareholders in proportion to their ownership and thus become part of their personal taxes. In the early days of a business, when losses are likely, the owners are able to obtain a tax benefit on their personal returns.

Even when the business turns profitable, the S-corporation status can confer a tax benefit on owners, since corporate tax rates may be higher than personal rates. Drawbacks include limita–tions on the number of shareholders and a restriction to one class of stock. Switching back and forth from a C corporation to an S corporation can get complicated — and costly in recomputed taxes and legal fees.

Advantages

Incorporating a business provides a number of clear advantages, including the following:

- *Legal protection.* In a legal sense, the corporation is a shield between you and the outside world. In the most dire circum-stances, if the business gets into serious financial trouble, it can file for protection under federal bankruptcy laws. These laws prevent creditors from coming after either the company's or the shareholders' assets.

  If the company can't be successfully reorganized and must be liquidated, the owners' personal assets can't usually be targeted by creditors and lenders to satisfy outstanding debts. It should be noted that there are exceptions to this protection, such as when the owners are judged to have been fraudulent. In addition, banks can come after officers for repayment of loans for which the officers signed a personal guarantee. Such guarantees are often required before banks will make loans to young companies.

- **Credibility.** A business that can add Inc. or Corp. after its name gains credibility that a sole proprietorship or partnership does not have. It suggests to potential customers, suppliers, and lenders a business that has achieved enough success that it needs to hire employees and has shareholders.

- **Flexibility.** Any number of approaches can be taken to capitalizing the corporation — setting up its financial underpinnings. Corporations can use debt, equity, or a combination of the two. Within these financial instruments are any number of variations that you have no doubt heard financial analysts refer to: convertible stock, preferred stock, warrants, common stock, debentures, and so on. These are tools to provide for such important issues as financing, estate planning, motivating employees, and taking the company public. Investors may want a combination of preferred stock and warrants in exchange for their funds. You may want to make common stock available as an incentive to certain employees to improve their performance or as a substitute for cash payments.

- **Benefits availability.** A corporation often has easier access to such benefits as accident, health, and life insurance for its employees. Moreover, these benefits can often be purchased at substantially discounted group rates.

- **Tax advantages.** As noted earlier in this section, S corporations often offer tax advantages to their shareholders. In addition, all corporations may have the advantage of enabling you to save income and estate taxes by making gifts of stock to your children.

Disadvantages

The benefits of a corporate organization come at some cost. The main disadvantages are as follows:

- *Potentially higher taxes.* As noted, corporate tax rates tend to be higher than personal rates. This disadvantage can be at least partially offset by organizing as an S corporation. But there may still be state taxes and fees on the corporation that you wouldn't pay if the company were a sole proprietorship or partnership.

- *Increased formality.* A corporation must have bylaws, a board of directors, and an annual meeting of shareholders, among other legal requirements. Certainly these formalities can be given lip service and the company run the way the owners prefer, but they shouldn't lose sight of the fact that the board of directors has real power. Not only does it select the officers (who may be the same as the directors), but it may be called on to make important decisions about the rights of minority shareholders, potential acquisitions, and other matters. As the company grows, it may add outsiders to the board — in effect, diminishing the power of the founders.

- *Increased legal fees.* The legalities of establishing a corporation should be handled by a knowledgeable attorney. But the involvement of attorneys doesn't end with the filing of incorporation papers. Shortly after, bylaws must be developed covering the election of directors, fees for directors, shareholder meeting dates, and so on. Many corporations continue to rely on their attorneys to remind them about annual meetings, assemble meeting minutes, monitor changes in shareholder lists, and file annual paperwork with state officials. Business attorneys know how to maintain these matters in their proper form, which becomes important if you ever want to sell the company and demonstrate to the potential buyers that the company has been operated correctly from a legal perspective.

• **Risk of minority shareholders.** Ownership in a corporation is easy to make available to others by simply selling or handing out stock. As noted in the previous chapter, many successful entrepreneurs advocate making stock available to key employees during the early days when cash is typically in short supply. The downside of making stock available to those outside the immediate circle of founders is that in the future you may wind up with unhappy or troublesome minority shareholders. Because they are in the minority, they can't govern the majority's decision-making power, but they can be a pain in the neck. The minority holders can request information about such matters as officer salaries, company contractors, and other business issues. If the minority holders feel they are being discriminated against, they can sue and in some cases force the majority to be more accommodating.

What to Do?

For any business with potential legal exposure (which is nearly any company selling a product and some service companies) or hopes of growing significantly or both, incorporating makes a lot of sense. It provides as much legal protection as is possible for the owners' personal assets. And it provides credibility and mechanisms for distributing ownership essential to attract outside financing and key employees.

But incorporating also presents entrepreneurs with a wider variety of options and variations than either a sole proprietorship or a partnership. To gain the maximum benefits possible from being incorporated, take special note of the following:

• **Hire a good attorney.**

The actual act of incorporating is essentially a mechanical one. But the decisions about such seemingly mundane matters as bylaws and boards of directors can have significant long-term implications. A good business attorney can provide advice on these subtle issues. Try to use an attorney who is sensitive to your long-term goals. Avoid the attorney who tells you incorporating is just a matter of filing a few papers. This is one area in which you want an attorney to take some time and explore the alternative structural matters with you.

• *Evaluate the C-corp. – S-corp. decision.*

This decision can have important ramifications. If you go with an S corporation, for instance, you may limit your ability to attract funds from a venture capital firm, since S-corp. regulations require that shareholders only be individuals. I don't want to evaluate the choice too closely, however, because regulations regarding S corporations have undergone some change in recent years and are likely to change further. Your attorney or accountant should be up to date on the regulations and able to advise you on the best choice at the time you are incorporating.

• *Come up with a rational capital structure.*

The way you set up your company's stock affects your flexibility in such areas as obtaining financing, rewarding employees, and doing estate planning. You may want to have a separate class of nonvoting stock, for example, to make available to key employees. This stock could grow in value but would prevent employees from having a say in such key matters as electing directors or determining officers' salaries.

• *Determine what role the board of directors will have.*

The most common decision is whether to bring individuals who aren't officers or paid professionals onto the board. I discussed some of the issues affecting boards earlier in this chapter, but the decision is an important one that should be discussed at the time incorporation is being considered.

■ In Conclusion

It's easy to tune out about the legal organizational issues that all entrepreneurs must deal with. Indeed, many of the decisions you make about organizing your company can be undone or altered as the business grows. But some of the decisions are difficult to undo or are costly in terms of taxes and legal fees.

Thinking carefully about the organization that will serve your new business best serves two other functions. First, it will likely save you time and aggravation later because you won't have to undo your mistakes. Second, it helps you think about your long-term plans for the business in such important areas as making stock available to employees, bringing on a panel of outside advisers, and seeking outside investors. These are part and parcel of the planning process, about which more is discussed in Chapter 8.

■ **Exercise I: Assessing Competitors**

1. Which legal structure is most common in your industry?

2. Explain why that structure is preferred.

3. Identify your key competitors' legal structures.

4. In your view, why did each competitor select its particular organizational structure?

5. How does this structure help your competitor?

6. How does this structure hurt your competitor?

■ Exercise II: Organizing Your Business

A. List the pros and cons of each of the three business organizing options listed below:

Sole Proprietorship	
Advantages	**Disadvantages**

Incorporation	
Advantages	**Disadvantages**

Partnership	
Advantages	**Disadvantages**

B. Select one of the three organizing options that best suits your new company's needs. List three reasons why this particular option will benefit you. For the other two structures, list three reasons why each structure would not prove advantageous.

Sole Proprietorship

_____

_____

_____

Incorporation

_____

_____

_____

Partnership

_____

_____

_____

YOUR CASH FLOW

"Cash flow is more important than your mother."
....
Anonymous

Nearly every successful entrepreneur has a tale about how his or her business almost ran out of money.

For Celestial Seasonings, as for many companies, that happened during its earliest days. The company was hand-packing its herbal tea in cloth bags, recalls founder Mo Siegel: "We were so broke, we couldn't even afford to have ties to close the bags. So we went to Ma Bell and asked if we could have its telephone scrap wire. If you have ever opened a cable of telephone wire, you see copper wire covered with multicolored plastic. So we would slice the cable like that, slit it open, and there would be these cute little red and pink and blue wires. We would use those to close the tops of the bags."

Celestial Seasonings didn't have the cash on hand to buy fancy ribbons or wires to close its bags of tea. Mo Siegel at that instant had two options: delay shipping the product (and lose the potential for desperately needed cash) or find another way to accomplish what needed to be accomplished.

I could spend many paragraphs explaining cash flow in dry technical terms, but it is from such experiences as that described by

Mo Siegel that one gets a true understanding of the meaning, and importance, of cash flow. Indeed, for many entrepreneurs cash flow is more *an experience* than an accounting or financial term — and it was probably an entrepreneur who had been through an unhappy cash-flow experience who came up with the quote at the beginning of this chapter.

However, on-the-job training in the meaning and ramifications of cash flow is a dangerous business. The war stories that such successful entrepreneurs as Mo Siegel and others tell about narrow escapes from cash binds are entertaining in retrospect. When told by failed entrepreneurs, though, such tales can be tearjerkers. Then the stories often end with something like, "If only I had had the cash. . . ."

Moreover, entrepreneurs who understand what cash flow means can use the concept to work for them to minimize dangerous situations. In this chapter I try to capture the meaning of cash flow in both emotional and technical terms.

■ What Is Cash Flow?

Quite simply, cash flow is the difference between the movement of money in and out of your business over a certain period of time — typically measured on a monthly or quarterly basis. When cash is in tight supply, though, entrepreneurs have been known to monitor cash flow on a weekly, daily, or even hourly basis.

In defining cash flow, it is important to avoid confusing it with other aspects of finance. Too often, cash flow is confused with sales and profits. Yet it is not an uncommon occurrence for a small company to make a significant sale or be operating on a profitable basis and go broke because of insufficient cash flow.

The problem may be that the price of the product or service is too low for the incoming cash to cover all the company's expenses. Or it may be that the company doesn't get paid for two, three, or four months after its product or service has been delivered. In the meantime, it runs out of cash because it doesn't have the funds to pay its ongoing expenses.

George Kachajian of Silicon Technology provides a succinct overview of cash flow: "The only way to run a business is based on cash flow, which is strictly a measure of the amount of cash flowing in and the amount of cash flowing out in a given time period — weekly, monthly, or whatever. The flow of cash is critical to your business because, when your bank balance at the end of the month is below zero, you are bankrupt, out of business. You have to have one dollar more than zero at the end of each period. . . . I know what my cash is daily."

■ Beyond Cash In/Cash Out

OK, you may be saying to yourself. So now I know that if I run out of cash, my business goes broke. It takes a whole chapter to explain that?

It turns out that there is more to cash flow than cash in/cash out. Analyzing and projecting cash flow serves as a powerful planning tool for a start-up and early-stage business. It can help you make some important determinations, including the following:

• *The minimum amount of cash you'll need for successful start-up.*

In its early days, a start-up business is spending much more than it is taking in. Cash-flow analysis can help you determine how much cash you'll need to provide before there's enough cash coming in to carry the business.

Kachajian used cash-flow projections for just this purpose to help guide his product development and sales planning: "In our case, I realized that I needed two years to develop my own manufacturing capability, and I estimated what that would cost in machinery and people — salaries as well as health and other benefits. I projected those numbers out over two years and worked it back as to how many machines I had to sell over that period of time and at what price. We needed to sell twenty machines in order to gain the time to develop the whole manufacturing capability. The only unknown was whether I would sell those twenty machines over that time period. So there we were. We had our homework done. We sell the twenty machines and we are successful, we have survived. If we don't, we are under." In other words, the necessary cash that Kachajian calculated was equal to the price of twenty machines.

• *How much outside financing the business may require.*

By projecting the amount of cash your business will have coming in and going out on a monthly basis for a year or two, it

CASH-FLOW TERMINOLOGY

I. STARTING CASH (starting balance). Each monthly projection begins with the amount of cash you have on hand at the start of the month. Your starting cash is the same number as the previous month's ending balance.

2. CASH IN. This section of the statement is also called sources of cash. It includes all cash received this month. There are several possible sources:

a. *Sales* are a primary source of cash, but remember to include only cash sales. Sales that have been invoiced do not represent money you can spend this month, so list here only the cash sales you expect to have.
b. *Paid Receivables* are those sales that were previously invoiced and have been paid this month. It is important to project accurately when you expect to be paid — thirty days, sixty days, etc. If a sale made in January is actually going to be collected in March, you want your projections to be realistic and reflect that lag time. You can't spend cash you haven't yet collected.
c. *Interest.* Should you be so fortunate as to have money in the bank, you'll be earning interest.
d. *Other*. Additional sources of cash might be a bank loan, a sale of stock, the sale of some asset such as a company car, or royalties from an invention.

is possible to determine how much money you may need to borrow from a bank or obtain from investors. Because you may want to start the business on a larger scale than what you can afford yourself, the amount you come up with here may be more than the amount you calculate in the previous section. In any event, a cash-flow analysis is an essential component of your request to financial sources for funds.

• *How you might make your existing cash last longer.*
    This is perhaps the most common use of cash-flow analysis

3. CASH OUT. This section is also referred to as uses of cash. Cash leaves the business in two basic ways: fixed expenses and variable expenses.

a. *Fixed expenses* are incurred regularly and cannot easily be eliminated. Some examples are rent and payroll, payroll taxes, estimated taxes, utilities, interest on loans, and insurance payments.
b. *Variable expenses* can change from month to month and often vary with sales volume or production volume. Generally, they can be more easily changed than fixed expenses. Some examples are supplies, commissions, advertising, raw materials, consulting services, and promotion.

4. ENDING BALANCE (or ending cash) is how much cash is left at the end of the month. It is the result of the numbers in the cash in and cash out columns. You simply add the starting cash to total cash in and then subtract total cash out. The cash you end the month with is the cash you have to start the next month — so you get the number for the starting cash column by simply copying it from the previous month's ending balance.

5. CASH FLOW is the amount of cash that has flowed through the business. It is a measure of change, of what has happened that month. If nothing has happened — if you begin with $1,000 and don't take any cash in or pay out a nickel, you would end with $1,000, but your cash flow would be zero. To calculate cash flow, subtract the total cash out from the total cash in.

by early-stage entrepreneurs. When cash isn't coming in as fast as they expected it would, they begin analyzing the cash flow — particularly the outflows — to determine how to get more out of the company's remaining cash. Mo Siegel got free wire to tie bags of tea. Some entrepreneurs move to cheaper offices. Others reduce the hours of full-time employees.

Entrepreneurs may also determine that inflows are lagging because too many customers are taking too long to pay their bills. Then they may move to tighten their credit policies or telephone slow payers more frequently. Whatever the action under consideration, cash-flow analysis makes clear the impact on future cash availability. Later in this chapter, I provide suggestions for getting more out of your cash based on the experiences of our entrepreneurs.

■ How Much Cash Do You Need for Start-up?

This is one of the first questions entrepreneurs want answered. There is, of course, no way of getting a definitive answer before opening the company's doors. But creating a monthly cash-flow statement for the first few months can give you as close an approximation as you are likely to get.

You'll find a standard cash-flow statement on which you can do your own calculations on page 125 (Table 1). The important items to note are a cash-flow statement's four main elements:

1. Cash on hand at the start of each quarter, month, week, etc. (starting cash).
2. Cash coming in (total cash in).
3. Cash going out (total cash out).
4. Cash left at the end of the month (ending balance).

Technically, the difference between items one and four is the cash flow, or change at the bottom of the cash-flow statement.

Two important matters to take note of at this point:

- **Stick to the rules.** Your cash-flow statement should be based on standard accounting techniques. Don't be creative in putting together a cash-flow statement or any other financial statement. For one thing, you'll run the risk of distorting the information you are trying to glean from the exercise. For another, you'll very quickly turn off any financial expert, such as a banker or venture capitalist. You can use the statement in Table 1 as a model, adding items as necessary to show other sources of cash in (i.e., interest from bank accounts, royalties, etc.) and cash out (advertising, equipment, supplies, etc.)

TABLE 1

STANDARD CASH FLOW STATEMENT

	Month 1	Month 2	Month 3	Month 4	Month 5	Month 6
STARTING CASH						
CASH IN						
Cash sales						
Collected receivables						
Other						
TOTAL CASH IN						
CASH OUT						
Rent						
Payroll						
Other						
TOTAL CASH OUT						
ENDING BALANCE						
CHANGE (Cash flow)						

• **Be realistic.** You've probably heard the computer-related truism, "Garbage in, garbage out." Well, the same thing applies to cash-flow statements. If the numbers you enter about receivables, rent, payroll, and other matters aren't realistic, then your cash-flow statement won't be realistic. Because entrepreneurs tend to be optimists, it's especially important that they discard the rose-colored glasses when putting together a cash-flow statement. Indeed, they should even go a step further and be pessimistic, at least temporarily.

The reality for a start-up business is that expenses tend to be higher and revenues lower than expected. Mo Siegel perhaps puts it best when he warns: "I hate to say this, because it sounds a little downcast, but it's going to cost more than you ever thought, it's going to be harder than you ever expected, it's going to be a lot worse than you ever imagined, it's going to be a total pain in the neck, so you had better make sure that there is extra cash built into it."

Another way of handling this potential problem is to do two or three cash-flow projections: a best case, worst case, and a likely case. Then you'll have a clearer sense of the possibilities.

With these advisories in mind, let's examine how to create a monthly cash-flow statement that will help determine the amount of money you will need for start-up. To illustrate the process, I use a hypothetical example, Your Business. (For definitions of the cash-flow terms, see the box, "Cash-Flow Terminology," on pages 120–121.) Remember, this is designed to get across lessons about cash flow rather than being about any particular kind of business and is intentionally a primer. Most businesses would have additional items entered under the cash in and cash out columns to reflect other likely sources of income and expenses. You can follow along by referring to Table 2 on page 125.

• **Cash in.** Because we want to determine how much money you are going to need, we start with a zero balance. Our first step is to turn to our sources of cash in. We begin with cash income, which comes from cash sales. If you expect to make $3,000 in sales this month, but only $1,000 is cash sales with the rest paid in 30 days, then only the cash should be recorded here. Payment that is due from customers but not yet received is called accounts receivable, or simply receivables.

After the first month, you will rightfully expect some of the receivables to be collected each month, so those will be added to the cash column for subsequent months (discussed later). Your total sales for the month received in cash are therefore $1,000.

Other sources of cash income for the month might be from a bank loan or from interest on bank accounts. But in this case you can expect no other such resources. So we simply add up these sources of income for a total of $1,000 cash in.

• **Cash out.** Now let's move to the cash out column. Cash leaves the business in two basic forms:

1. **Fixed expenses.** These are expenses that must be paid regularly and can't easily be eliminated. In our example, these include $700 rent and $1,000 of payroll. You will need to create your own checklist of expenses to run through each month. Are quarterly taxes due this month? Any insurance payments? Each business will have its own list of expenses.

TABLE 2: STARTING OUT	
CASH FLOW/ YOUR BUSINESS	
	Month 1
STARTING CASH	$ 0
CASH IN	
Cash sales	1,000
Collected receivables	0
Other	0
TOTAL CASH IN	1,000
CASH OUT	
Rent	700
Payroll	1,000
Other	300
TOTAL CASH OUT	2,000
ENDING BALANCE	(1,000)
CHANGE (Cash flow)	($ 1,000)

2. Variable expenses. Those are expenses that change, or vary, from month to month — often in accordance with sales levels — and can be more easily cut or added to than fixed expenses. Variable expenses might include supplies, advertising and promotion, and consulting services. In our example, we will say that variable expenses for month 1 are $300 in supplies.

- **Cash flow.** We now total up the cash out column to get $2,000 cash out in month 1. Our ending balance for the month is calculated by simply adding our starting balance of zero dollars to total cash in of $1,000 and then subtracting the $2,000 total cash out. Our ending balance is therefore a negative $1,000. We also want to calculate our cash flow — the change between our beginning balance and ending balance. We went from zero dollars to negative $1,000, so our cash flow was negative $1,000 for this month.

- **The key number.** Believe it or not, all this detail is moving us toward the key number — the amount you'll need to start-up. To actually tabulate it, though, we need to repeat the process described for month 1 for additional months. So at this point, we move to Table 3 on page 127 to show projections for future months. To begin month 2, we take month 1's ending balance of negative $1,000 and make it our starting balance for month 2. In Table 3, we carry out this cash flow for six months.

    In order to determine how much start-up capital you will need, you must continue the cash-flow projection until you are sure your ending balance is positive. For most businesses, we would look at cash flow for a year or two to be sure our cash flow is staying positive. In our example, we will assume this healthy business shows a reliably positive ending balance by month 6.

    We then look back over all our ending balances to find the largest negative balance. It occurs in month 2, a negative $2,500. This number tells us how much start-up cash we need to keep the business going until break-even — until all our expenses are covered and we are making money.

Note what happens when we redo our cash flow in Table 4 on page 129 with the $2,500 start-up cash. Our ending balance in month 1 changes from negative $1,000 to positive $1,500.

Because our ending balance has changed, the beginning balance for the following month must also change. The new ending balance for month 2, which was our maximum negative ending balance, now becomes zero dollars. We have used up all our cash, but we have also paid all our obligations this month.

TABLE 3: DETERMINING START-UP CASH-FLOW NEEDS

CASH FLOW/YOUR BUSINESS

	Month 1	Month 2	Month 3	Month 4	Month 5	Month 6
STARTING CASH	$0	($1,000)	($2,500)	($2,200)	($400)	$2,900
CASH IN						
Cash sales	1,000	1,500	3,000	4,000	5,000	5,000
Collected receivables	0	500	1,000	1,500	2,500	2,500
Other	—	—	—	—	—	—
TOTAL CASH IN	1,000	2,000	4,000	5,500	7,500	7,500
CASH OUT						
Rent	700	700	700	700	700	700
Payroll	1,000	2,500	2,500	2,500	2,500	2,500
Other	300	300	500	500	1,000	1,500
TOTAL CASH OUT	2,000	3,500	3,700	3,700	4,200	4,700
ENDING BALANCE	(1,000)	(2,500)	(2,200)	(400)	2,900	5,700
CHANGE (Cash flow)	($1,000)	($1,500)	$300	$1,800	$3,300	$2,800

Keeping in mind that each ending balance becomes the next month's beginning balance, you can see what happens in the following months. Month 2 is still our lowest point, but none of our ending balances are negative. We will have enough cash to pay all our bills and to meet our payroll — provided that our assumptions about the size of expenses and the success of our sales efforts are in fact accurate.

Note that while the beginning and ending balances have all changed, cash flow has remained the same. This is because the actual flow of cash in and out each month has not changed.

■ How Much Financing Do You Need?

In the previous example, you were determining how much it would cost you to start the business yourself. So the scale of the business allowed for what you could reasonably hope to accomplish from your own savings. But it could be that you've determined that Your Business would have much greater long-term profit potential if it were started on a larger scale. To do so, though, would require some help from outside lenders and/or investors. The key question is, How much help?

In the cash-flow projection for Your Business in Table 5 on page 132, the company has been enlarged so that rent is $1,200 monthly instead of $700 and other expenses are considerably higher. We also assume that the larger presence stimulates sales to a much greater degree by month 4.

Here we see that the amount required to start the business is $4,600, as registered in the ending balance at the end of month 3. Since you only have $2,500, the amount of financing required is $2,100. Having done this analysis, you would be able to make a fairly convincing case to a lender or investor that you had done your homework to demonstrate your need for financing. Potential lenders or investors may take issue about your estimates, but at least you'd be talking and perhaps even negotiating rather than wondering why they wouldn't even talk with you.

■ Stretching Your Cash

Cash-flow projections of the type used to illustrate start-up and financing needs can also be used to help you figure out ways to make your cash go further. Basically, there are two approaches:

• *Cutting cash outflows.* There are lots of ways to cut the amount of cash flowing out of your business. You can scout out cheaper suppliers. You might try to find lower-rent quarters. If things get really tight, you can reduce your staff's hours or numbers.

Returning to Your Company, we can see in Table 6 on page 135 the effect of postponing the hiring of a second employee in

TABLE 4: START-UP CASH ON HAND

CASH FLOW/YOUR BUSINESS

	Month 1	Month 2	Month 3	Month 4	Month 5	Month 6
STARTING CASH	$2,500	$1,500	$0	$300	$2,100	$5,400
CASH IN						
Cash sales	1,000	1,500	3,000	4,000	5,000	5,000
Collected receivables	0	500	1,000	1,500	2,500	2,500
Other						
TOTAL CASH IN	1,000	2,000	4,000	5,000	7,500	7,500
CASH OUT						
Rent	700	700	700	700	700	700
Payroll	1,000	2,500	2,500	2,500	2,500	2,500
Other	300	300	500	500	1,000	1,500
TOTAL CASH OUT	2,000	3,500	3,700	3,700	4,200	4,700
ENDING BALANCE	1,500	0	300	2,100	5,400	8,200
CHANGE (Cash flow)	($1,000)	($1,500)	$300	$1,800	$3,300	$2,800

month 2 until month 5. Our payroll expense goes from $2,500 to $1,000 for months 2, 3, and 4. Our total cash out is changed in those months and all ending balances and subsequent beginning balances are changed. The net result is that we get a positive ending balance in month 3 instead of waiting until month 5.

• *Increasing cash inflows.* Less obvious is how to increase the amount of cash coming in beyond simply selling more. One way that entrepreneurs sometimes overlook is to increase the speed in which you are paid by customers. If a customer pays his or her bill in 30 days rather than 60 days, you have access to the cash 30 days sooner.

We can get a clear indication of the impact of speeding collections by looking once again at the original version of Your Business in Table 7 on page 136. If we assume that we can speed up our collected receivables by $500 each month, our total cash in also increases by $500 each month. Each ending balance is changed by this and each subsequent beginning balance is also changed. In month 4, our ending balance has gone from a negative $400 to a positive $1,100 — simply by increasing the speed with which the business collects the money it is owed. Once again, be sure that all assumptions and changes in your cash flow are as realistic as possible.

■ Tips for Getting More Out of Your Cash

Based on the exercises we just went through, it's easy to conclude that overcoming many of the cash-flow obstacles of a start-up business's early days is a numbers game. The more you can squeeze out of your cash, the better off you are. That is true but only to a point. Your efforts to get more out of your cash must be balanced against the need of the business to produce a quality product or provide a quality service. For instance, you may conclude that by cutting your employees' pay, you can stretch your cash an extra few months. But cutting their pay may make them resentful and less productive, resulting in product defects or inferior service to customers.

Here are some suggestions offered by the entrepreneurs we interviewed about effective ways to stretch your cash in the start-up days:

- **Watch your overhead.** Some entrepreneurs, feeling flush because of the savings, investment, or other start-up funds they have in hand, decide that their business has to "go first class" to present an appearance of success to outsiders. So they go overboard in acquiring store or office space or buying furniture and equipment. Yet it may be possible to achieve the same results at lower cost, as George Kachajian did in his start-up days. "In the beginning, I would look in the papers for auctions on other businesses that went under. I believe the table we are sitting at here was purchased at an auction of a company that opened world headquarters in November of a given year and went bankrupt in February. Apparently, they didn't have a cash-flow projection."

    It's also easy for new companies to be deluded by early initial success and become inattentive to their expenses, says Crate & Barrel's Gordon Segal. "You have to be very cost conscious in what you do, even when you start getting initially successful. The expenses start running away with themselves, and soon entrepreneurs discover that their expenses exceed their incomes and suddenly they are in financial difficulty. They just don't control the business. No matter how much initial capital you have, you need to be very careful about how it is spent. You cannot let your expenses exceed your income. You have to create a sense with your vendors and your associates who work with you that this has to be."

- **Negotiate on price.** Most of the successful entrepreneurs we interviewed point out that they had little reluctance to take every opportunity to try to negotiate lower prices. Confides Mo Siegel: "My biggest secret was always being a good buyer. I am a tough buyer and I am a tough negotiator. If they tell me it cost $3, I don't mind telling a store I only have $2, I am sorry. I don't mind bartering. I don't mind bartering on fixed prices if I am really against the wall. No problem."

Frank Carney seconds that approach: "It never hurts to use, 'Boy, I am just starting out. I don't have a lot of money and I can't afford this, but I sure like this.' It is the old negotiating game."

- *Maintain good relations with your vendors.* Vendors from whom you obtain regularly required supplies and services can also be helpful in improving your cash flow. One vendor who will sell to

TABLE 5: STARTING BIGGER

CASH FLOW/YOUR BUSINESS

	Month 1	Month 2	Month 3	Month 4	Month 5	Month 6
STARTING CASH	$0	($1,800)	($4,100)	($4,600)	($2,600)	$2,700
CASH IN						
Cash sales	1,000	1,500	3,000	5,000	7,000	9,000
Collected receivables	0	500	1,000	1,500	3,000	4,000
Other						
TOTAL CASH IN	1,000	2,000	4,000	6,500	10,000	13,000
CASH OUT						
Rent	1,200	1,200	1,200	1,200	1,200	1,200
Payroll	1,000	2,500	2,500	2,500	2,500	2,500
Other	600	600	800	800	1,000	1,500
TOTAL CASH OUT	2,800	4,300	4,500	4,500	4,700	5,200
ENDING BALANCE	(1,800)	(4,100)	(4,600)	(2,600)	2,700	10,500
CHANGE (Cash flow)	($1,800)	($2,300)	($500)	$2,000	$5,300	$7,800

you on 30 days credit may be more valuable than a competitor who offers lower prices but requires payment on delivery. Similarly, a vendor who will reliably deliver goods on a timely basis can help save your business cash by reducing the amount of inventory you need to maintain on hand.

Here is how Carney explains the dilemma: "You want a certain quality and you want the most competitive price, and you want to be sure you get the service that matches what service you are promising to your customers. It doesn't matter at all if you get a great price and then get service and delivery terms that you cannot deal with. You have to get it to match what your space is for storage, what your capability is financially. It is best to get delivery just in time for production so that you minimize the inventory that you have in your store. It doesn't matter what kind of store it is. In order to do that, you have to have a good relationship with that supplier and you have to pick your suppliers based on what kind of service they can give. You have to study all those factors in order to make the determination."

- **Be careful about extending credit.** Start-up entrepreneurs are particularly vulnerable to unforeseen cash problems stemming from bad credit. Because start-up entrepreneurs are so eager to make those initial sales, little attention is typically given to checking the credit history or capacity of potential customers. Christine Martindale of Esprit Miami stumbled in this area during her first year in business: "I was honest and I expected that customers would pay me. I had a lot of people who didn't pay me the first year. I lost in that year four times my entire investment." In retrospect, she says she would have hired or used the services of a bookkeeper who could have asked potential customers for credit references and/or used the services of a credit agency that keeps tabs on companies' credit histories. Paying such agencies is usually money well spent.

- **Seek upfront payments.** One good way to test out the likelihood of collecting from a customer seeking credit is to ask for an upfront payment equal to one-fourth, one-third, or one-half of the amount of the sale. You might also seek to schedule the balance due to be paid in regular installments on certain agreed-on dates. A poor credit risk will probably refuse both options. Once customers establish a track record of paying on schedule, you can choose to forego the upfront payments.

- **Aggressively collect receivables.** Even customers who can pay will often try to take as much time as possible to come up with the cash. If they can use your credit, it will be cheaper than what a bank would charge. Your challenge is to avoid serving as banker to your customers. There are a number of approaches to speed collection of receivables. One is simply to get on the telephone the day after your bill comes due; if you allow 30 days for payment, you should be on the phone to the customer on day 31. Another technique is to provide a discount of some kind — typically 1% to 3% — to those customers who pay within some specified time, say 10 or 15 days. The main drawback to this approach is that some customers who pay after the specified time will take the discount anyway, so you may have to experiment to determine if it works for you. Alternately, you can charge interest of 1% to 2% monthly to customers who are late payers. Usually the best approach is to regularly contact late payers by phone; if they make a habit of delaying, then you may have to decide if the customer is valuable enough to justify the late payment or if you should refuse to sell to that customer.

- **Exercise care in your pricing.** Along with being too easy on extending credit, start-up entrepreneurs are often unrealistic about the prices they charge — erring on the side of charging too little. In the service area, this is an especially common trap, as James Lowry can tell you: "We made some mistakes early on that could have cost us dearly. We overpromised in terms of what we would give a client in the length of the analysis, the number of hours invested on site, the quality of the report, the number of pages. We were kind of naive in terms of how many hours would that take of my time and staff time to produce that. We looked up at the end of one project and the client was just ecstatic over our work, and the accountant looked at how much we charged and said we lost money on the deal. It was trial and error. It didn't cost us so dearly that we bellied up, but it cost us in terms of profitability. Now I think we are pretty secure in how we scope out projects." His point, though, is that a company that underprices itself can seem

TABLE 6: CUTTING EXPENSES

CASH FLOW: YOUR BUSINESS

	Month 1	Month 2	Month 3	Month 4	Month 5	Month 6
STARTING CASH	$0	($1,000)	($1,000)	$800	$4,100	$7,400
CASH IN						
Cash sales	1,000	1,500	3,000	4,000	5,000	5,000
Collected receivables	0	500	1,000	1,500	2,500	2,500
Other						
TOTAL CASH IN	1,000	2,000	4,000	5,500	7,500	7,500
CASH OUT						
Rent	700	700	700	700	700	700
Payroll	1,000	1,000	1,000	1,000	2,500	2,500
Other	300	300	500	500	1,000	1,500
TOTAL CASH OUT	2,000	2,000	2,200	2,200	4,200	4,700
ENDING BALANCE	(1,000)	(1,000)	800	4,100	7,400	10,200
CHANGE (Cash flow)	($1,000)	$0	$1,800	$3,300	$3,300	$2,800

to be doing great because it is very busy and then suddenly find itself running short of cash. Conducting cash-flow analyses can help you anticipate such a problem before it catches the business by surprise.

- *Don't compromise your company's image.* In their zeal to trim costs, some entrepreneurs inadvertently cut into items essential to creating the intangible attraction that is the heart of a company's appeal to customers. Gordon Segal explains the notion well, after pointing out how hardheaded he has always been in watching pennies. "We never accepted a first price on something. We

TABLE 7: SPEEDING COLLECTIONS

YOUR BUSINESS/CASH FLOW WORKSHEET

	Month 1	Month 2	Month 3	Month 4	Month 5	Month 6
STARTING CASH	$0	($1,000)	($2,000)	($1,200)	$1,100	$4,900
CASH IN						
Cash sales	1,000	1,500	3,000	4,000	5,000	5,000
Collected receivables	0	1,000	1,500	2,000	3,000	3,000
Other						
TOTAL CASH IN	1,000	2,500	4,500	6,000	8,000	8,000
CASH OUT						
Rent	700	700	700	700	700	700
Payroll	1,000	2,500	2,500	2,500	2,500	2,500
Other	300	300	500	500	1,000	1,000
TOTAL CASH OUT	2,000	3,500	3,700	3,700	4,200	4,200
ENDING BALANCE	(1,000)	(2,000)	(1,200)	1,100	4,900	8,700
CHANGE (Cash flow)	($1,000)	($1,000)	$800	$2,300	$3,800	$3,800

always said there is another price. Now what is it?. . . . It is very important to be cost conscious of everything and not let the artistic part of us overwhelm the business part. Yet we often say in our business that it is a mix between an arts one and a business one. It is a very narrow line. If we are too artistic and don't watch the costs of running the business efficiently, we won't be in business. On the other hand, if we are too much of a business, we won't have a unique enough or colorful enough presentation or group of people who are good enough to run the beautiful store. So it is that very fine line that you have to maintain."

Frank Carney makes this observation: "Saving money in the beginning of a business by buying as cheap as you can is good for everybody, but you have got to remember that some businesses are really geared to a certain style of consumer and a certain flair, and you have to make investments to get that flair. If you have a barber/beauty shop in a mall shopping center and it is supposed to look different than the normal barber/beauty shop, and if you save by buying used equipment and put cheap carpeting in and cheap this and cheap that, you might save a lot of money, but you wouldn't have the pizzazz of that business."

■ Exercise I: Cash Flow Projection

Using a cash-flow projection for the next six months, determine how much start-up money ABC New Business will require. Base your projection on the following assumptions:

- Cash sales begin at $5,000 monthly the first two months and increase by $3,000 in month 3 and $2,000 a month thereafter.

- Collected receivables are $1,000 each in months 2 and 3, and increase by $1,000 monthly thereafter.

- Rent is $3,000 a month.

- Two employees are hired at salaries of $24,000 a year each, paid on a monthly basis.

- Supplies cost $2,000 the first month and increase $1,000 a month until month 3; they stay the same as month 3 thereafter.

(The answer can be found on page 140.)

■ Exercise II: Quiz

Answer true or false to the following statements:

1. The largest source of cash in to a business is usually generated by sales. T F

2. Dollar amounts appearing within parentheses on the cash-flow analysis depict a negative amount. T F

3. Each month's starting balance is derived from the previous month's ending balance. T F

4. Contracts that allow you to receive payments in installments are not a good idea, as accountants prefer to see businesses receive payments in one-lump sums. T F

5. Paying a credit service to check a potential
customer's credit rating is a waste of time and money.   T   F

6. Avoid telling clients who are delinquent paying
their bills that you cannot carry them. They may
assume you are near bankruptcy.   T   F

7. Stock up on items you do not need immediately.
This will save you time and money.   T   F

8. Fixed expenses are not paid regularly.   T   F

9. The word *profit* refers to the amount of
money that comes in and goes out of your
business over a set period of time.   T   F

10. Fixed expenses include items such
as office supplies and advertising fees.   T   F

11. Entrepreneurs should not hesitate to barter,
even when the price is "fixed."   T   F

12. Variable expenses include rent,
taxes, payroll, and insurance.   T   F

13. The break-even point occurs when all expenses
are covered and the company is making money.   T   F

14. In order to determine the amount of start-up funding
required for a business, entrepreneurs must perform
a cash-flow analysis until the ending balance is positive.   T   F

15. The term *accounts receivable* refers to the
amount of money the entrepreneur owes creditors.   T   F

16. Maintaining a policy of just-in-time inventory
requires an excellent relationship with your supplier.   T   F

ABC NEW BUSINESS CASH-FLOW PROJECTION
CASH-FLOW WORKSHEET

	Month 1	Month 2	Month 3	Month 4	Month 5	Month 6
STARTING CASH	$0	($4,000)	($8,000)	($10,000)	($9,000)	($5,000)
CASH IN						
Cash sales	5,000	5,000	8,000	10,000	12,000	14,000
Collected receivables		1,000	1,000	2,000	3,000	4,000
Other						
TOTAL CASH IN	5,000	6,000	9,000	12,000	15,000	18,000
CASH OUT						
Rent	3,000	3,000	3,000	3,000	3,000	3,000
Payroll	4,000	4,000	4,000	4,000	4,000	4,000
Supplies	2,000	3,000	4,000	4,000	4,000	4,000
TOTAL CASH OUT	9,000	10,000	11,000	11,000	11,000	11,000
ENDING BALANCE	(4,000)	(8,000)	(10,000)	(9,000)	(5,000)	2,000
CHANGE (Cash flow)	($4,000)	($4,000)	$2,000	$1,000	$4,000	$7,000

(ABC New Business will require $10,000 of start-up money based on projections for the first six months; the ending balance of negative $10,000 at the end of month 3 is the highest.)

Answers to Exercise II

1. True; 2. True; 3. True; 4. False; 5. False; 6. False; 7. False; 8. False; 9. False; 10. False; 11. True; 12. False; 13. False; 14. True; 15. False; 16. True

CHAPTER SEVEN

FINDING THE MONEY

"People who go to banks often get rejected,
as authors do when they write novels. Please don't be
concerned about the rejection. Find the better bank."

Art Snyder, vice chairman, US Trust Corp.

One of the great ironies about the way the press reports on small business is that banks and venture capitalists get an inordinate amount of attention as sources of start-up capital for new businesses. I wish I had a nickel for every article that has come out over the last ten years about how entrepreneurs should approach banks and venture capitalists for funding their new or growing businesses.

If you talk to successful entrepreneurs, you discover that very few of them obtained their start-up funds from a bank or venture capitalist. Indeed, none of the founders interviewed for this book started with financing from either a bank or a venture capital firm. That isn't to say they didn't at some point after start-up obtain bank or venture funds. But not at the very beginning.

Mo Siegel's tale of how Celestial Seasonings obtained its start-up financing, which follows up on the cash-flow problems he described at the start of the previous chapter, is not unusual. After the first year, when the company literally existed hand-to-mouth by obtaining telephone cable for tea-bag closures and finding its herbs growing wild in the woods ("You couldn't be more poor than we were," he recalls), a major turn of events occurred. "I teamed up with someone who had $800. That was like a major jump forward."

He adds, half-jokingly, "One of the things an entrepreneur can do is start with a high-finance deal like ours. Get a partner who can really bankroll it."

Actually, though, that $800 turned out to be pivotal. "We took the $800 and we borrowed money from a bank — $5,000. The banker was pretty skeptical that we were going to build a big company whose leading product was going to be Red Zinger herb tea. So he required that my partner's mother sign the bank loan [to personally guarantee repayment]. She did so willingly. Now, if she hadn't signed the bank loan, I think we could have still got the money, but it would have been tough. There is always a way, but you have to find it. It's that simple."

Having obtained the $5,000 loan, the fledgling company was able to raise an additional $5,000 by selling some of its stock to outside investors.

■ The Realities of the Financial Marketplace

What's the message in the experience of Mo Siegel and other entrepreneurs with similar tales of scraping together start-up funds? There are really several messages.

- *Expect skittishness from formal lenders and investors.* Institutional sources of money — especially banks and venture capital firms — don't want to be the first in with a loan or investment to a start-up business. They want evidence that the founding entrepreneur and/or family members, friends, and partners have put money into the business initially.

- *Start close to home.* A second, related message is that when you are just starting out, your best sources of financing are those closest to home. To spend lots of time and energy going to banks and venture capital firms during your company's earliest days may be a waste of precious resources that could be better devoted to concentrating on your company.

- *Expect to pay formal sources a high price.* Once you secure some close-to-home funds and look to banks and venture capitalists, expect these sources to exact a high price for their money. Banks typically want personal guarantees from the owners or relatives of the owners (such as from the mother of Mo Siegel's partner) so that if the loan isn't repaid, they can go after the real estate, stocks, and other personal property of those who signed the loan. Venture capitalists want a large chunk of ownership in a start-up company — 50% to 70% is not unheard of — assuming they are even interested in getting involved.

- *Evaluate whether you need less start-up money than you initially think.* Though Mo Siegel jokes about the $800 of start-up capital he obtained, the relatively small amount he was dealing with is not unusual among start-up entrepreneurs. An *Inc.* Magazine survey in 1989 of *Inc.* 500 chief executives — the heads of the most successful private companies in America — revealed that one-third started with less than $10,000 and nearly 70% began with under $50,000.

- *Consider the big picture.* The larger message is this: Loans and investments can come from two types of sources — those close to home and institutions. The rest of this chapter is organized with a view to those two sources.

■ Close-to-Home Money

This is money that, just as the title suggests, comes from sources as personal and close to home as the entrepreneur's own bank account. Surveys about sources of new-business financing consistently show that successful entrepreneurs rely most on sources that tend to get little attention in the press.

It's easy to understand why close-to-home sources don't get a lot of consideration: They are very hard to monitor and measure. While there are government and/or trade associations that keep track of the amount of bank lending and venture capital investing going on, there aren't any organizations that tabulate how much is borrowed from friends or via credit cards to start businesses. As a result, these resources don't get talked about much.

But, as the study of *Inc.* 500 companies mentioned in the previous section demonstrates, the close-to-home resources are an extremely critical part of the financing equation. (See Table 1 on the next page.) As just one example of the contrast between close-to-home money and institutional funding, note that the entrepreneur's own cash was most important or a significant source for three-fourths of the entrepreneurs, while venture capital was in the same categories for only 4% of the entrepreneurs.

Here are some of the most important close-to-home sources, along with a discussion of some of the issues they raise for entrepreneurs getting started:

- **Personal funds.** Ideally, start-up entrepreneurs want to use OPM — other people's money. And well they should. Most of us prefer to take a risk using money that isn't our own. Then the consequences of failure are less personally injurious.

  The fact of the matter is, it's nearly always essential for start-up entrepreneurs to commit at least some of their own money to a new venture. Even if they are among the select 4% who succeed in obtaining venture capital as a major source of start-up money, they will likely have to put some of their own money in to demonstrate their commitment to the venture.

  For many entrepreneurs, their own money is all they have when starting a business. That was the case for Jim Buck, founder of Northern Timber Framing, a builder of oak-timber homes in Cleveland. "I worked another job in the construction/engineering background, and I saved a lot from that," he said. "I have done a lot of my own labor, my own work in starting out, and just saved tooth and nail and put everything on the line. When it comes to it, that's how you get your money and how you get your start-up."

Personal savings aren't necessarily limited to the money you have in a bank account. James Lowry of James Lowry Associates discovered when he left his job as a consultant with a major firm that he had accumulated a significant amount of funds in a profit-sharing plan. Theoretically, that money was intended to be rolled over into a retirement account, but Lowry decided to use it as his start-up capital. That was not a terribly risky approach, since

WHERE INC. 500 COMPANIES RECEIVED FINANCING				
RESOURCE	**Most of $ from source**	**A significant source**	**A little**	**Did not use**
Own resources, cash	56%	19%	20%	5%
Mortgage of own assets	18%	17%	5%	60%
Charge cards	5%	5%	16%	74%
Other personal loans from bank	11%	12%	14%	63%
Spouse	4%	4%	5%	87%
Parents and/or other relative	8%	12%	12%	68%
Friend or business colleague	3%	6%	7%	84%
Partner	15%	14%	15%	56%
Another company	5%	5%	3%	86%
Bank (corp. loan)	19%	14%	8%	59%
Venture capital	2%	2%	1%	94%
Informal	3 %	5 %	2 %	90 %

having that money or not having it wouldn't be noticed for many years down the road.

The downside of committing all your savings, of course, is that if the business fails, you may be in a precarious personal financial position — having to begin a job search with no reserve funds at hand.

• **Personal borrowing.** I include in this category several types of loans individuals have fairly easy access to: loans against life insurance, credit cards, second mortgages, and personal bank loans. The potential yield from such loans can range widely.

Life insurance. Depending on how much life insurance you have (in whole-life rather than term-life policies) and how long you have had it, you may be able to borrow from $1,000 or $2,000 on up to $50,000 or $100,000. Interest rates are usually quite reasonable — ranging from 5% to 12%, depending on the policy's terms. The risk in borrowing against life insurance is fairly minimal; typically, you need only continue paying the interest on the loan along with the annual premium to keep the policy in effect. If you don't repay the loan principal, then the amount of the loan is deducted from the policy amount paid to your survivors should you die.

Credit cards. The keen competition among credit-card companies has made it reasonably easy for individuals to accumulate four, five, or more credit cards — each with a credit line of $5,000 to $10,000. You don't have to be a mathematical genius to see that it's possible to put together $50,000 of financing without too much trouble. Indeed, more than a quarter of the entrepreneurs surveyed by *Inc.* did use credit cards for at least some of their start-up financing.

The downside of credit cards is twofold. First, the interest rates are nearly usurious, on the order of 15% to 18% or more annually. That is very expensive money. Second, if you fail to pay the money back, you will have to deal with bill collectors and will likely wind up with a blemished credit record, which will make it difficult to get any other type of credit for five or more years.

Second mortgages. This is perhaps the most deceptive form of financing available — deceptive because it seems so easy to obtain and can be so dangerous in its long-term impact. A second mortgage is a loan against some portion of the equity in your house over and above what is owed on a first mortgage. Because many people have built up substantial equity in their homes, it is often possible to get a second mortgage for $50,000 to $200,000 or more. The interest rates are typically only 1% to 2% over the prime rate, and the interest is deductible from federal income taxes. Many banks and other financial institutions have marketed second mortgages quite aggressively, leading many an entrepreneur to ask, what could be easier?

The problem with second mortgages is that your home is the collateral for the loan. If the business you are starting with that money fails, you still have to keep making payments on the loan at a time when you can ill afford to. Failure to keep up with the payments means that the lender can foreclose on your home and sell it, using the proceeds to repay the loan. Thus, losing your business could also mean losing your home — a hardly insignificant risk.

Yet many entrepreneurs are willing to take that risk. As the *Inc.* survey showed, 35% of the entrepreneurs mortgaged their assets to obtain a significant portion of their start-up money.

Personal bank loan. It's possible for an entrepreneur to borrow money from a bank simply as an individual. This may seem like a nice way around the obstacles start-up companies typically face in going for bank loans, and sometimes it is. The catch is that you nearly always have to pledge collateral of some sort — stock, life insurance, real estate holdings, or savings account funds. If the business fails and you are unable to repay the loan, you can expect to lose the collateral. In addition, you may be forced to repay part of the loan if the value of the collateral decreases, such as in a stock market or real estate market decline.

The advantage of such a loan is you can obtain money without having to liquidate personal assets that are important to you (like life insurance) or that you believe will continue to increase in value (such as stock and real estate). The *Inc.* survey showed that nearly one-half of the businesses had made use of personal bank loans.

• *Family and friends.* Money from parents, in-laws, spouses, and friends is a bit like forbidden fruit — oh, so tempting but with hidden dangers. More often than not, these people want to help you. But because they are personally close to you, it's easy for emotional considerations to get in the way of a business transaction.

How so? The relatives may expect you to be eternally grateful — and to demonstrate your gratitude eternally. You may have a tendency to treat the money you receive from relatives with less seriousness than money from banks or venture capitalists in terms of repayment or providing a reasonable return.

Ideally, you should either treat the relationship as business-like as you would any other investment relationship, or you and your relatives should understand up front that this is an informal arrangement between people who care a lot for one another but aren't going to let the outcome influence the relationship long term. Frank Carney of Pizza Hut explains the latter attitude well when he observes that entrepreneurs he doesn't know well who approach him for money are often unrealistic about the high returns he expects as an investor. "That's why I often suggest that they get the money from friends and relatives, because friends and relatives will put up with [insufficient returns]. If my daughter comes to me and says, 'Let me have a couple thousand dollars to start a business,' I would do that as a father. . . . I wouldn't care what the return is because that is the way I am making that decision."

Some entrepreneurs feel more comfortable obtaining money from family than friends, apparently on the theory that you risk losing valued friends while close relatives will always be there. Christine Martindale, who obtained $5,000 of start-up funds from her mother to start Esprit Miami, says, "I think you can go to your family in certain instances. I wouldn't go to a friend because if you lose the money, then you lose the friend."

But as in the case of other risky financing sources, personal sources are popular with start-up entrepreneurs. The *Inc.* survey showed that more than 60% have made use of a spouse, relative, or friend/business colleague for start-up funding.

- **Angels.** These are wealthy individuals — often successful entrepreneurs who have sold their businesses for lots of cash — who like to invest in start-up or early-stage companies. It gives them an opportunity to again become involved in entrepreneurial situations, which they typically relish, as well as a chance to score big financially.

  Unfortunately, many entrepreneurs fail to understand the financial motivations of angels — thinking of them as angels too much in the giving sense. Frank Carney has been in the angel role since Pizza Hut was sold to Pepsico for $300 million during the 1980s, and he describes the misconceptions start-up entrepreneurs often have:

  "For every ten deals I take, six or seven are not going to work. So in the three or four that work — let's say my batting average is .333 — they have to have incredibly high returns on investment. But each entrepreneur who faces me and wants money and support doesn't want to give me my high return. . . . I need to get the possibility of making five, six, eight, or ten times my money to make up for the high percentage of deals that don't work . . . . I can't tell you how many times people will come to me and say that you can borrow at prime, at 8 $^1/2$% or whatever, and they think it's great if I get a 12% return on my money. I cannot afford an entrepreneurial deal of 12%. I can afford to put my money in the bank at 12%, but I cannot afford to risk it in an entrepreneurial venture where I lose two out of three times."

I can't explain the situation much better than that. If you are approaching individual investors, be prepared to sell them on all the money they stand to make from your company succeeding.

Be aware, though, that individual investors aren't all as bottom-line oriented as Carney suggests. Research on angels done by William Wetzel, a professor of finance at the University of New Hampshire, has shown that these individuals will sometimes accept a lower rate of return than traditional investors would take, especially if they think your business will create jobs and otherwise help the local economy.

In my experience, angels are also influenced by what I call "the showbiz factor." Certain types of businesses seem glamorous to individual investors — magazines, movies, nightclubs, sports-related businesses — to the point that they will accept additional risk or lower prospective returns in exchange for a chance to be in the limelight.

While some angels will invest individually, others like to invest in small groups through private offerings or limited partnerships. These are essentially ways of pooling funds. For guidance on using these vehicles, consult with an accountant and/or an attorney with experience in these areas. To make sure they have the necessary experience, don't be shy about asking for references of other entrepreneurs they have worked with, since putting together a private offering or limited partnership requires extensive experience and skill.

■ Institutional Sources

One of the most significant business trends in recent years has been the upheaval in America's financial marketplace. This upheaval has made much of the conventional wisdom about financing moot. Moreover, it has introduced all kinds of new players into the financing game.

It wasn't that long ago that entrepreneurs in search of financing beyond that discussed in the previous section — family, friends, life insurance policies — went to banks or venture capital firms. But by the beginning of the 1990s, both banks and venture capital firms had stumbled badly. Too many banks made too many bad real estate loans, and more than a few failed. Venture capital firms had made too many investments during the 1980s that weren't paying off at the start of the 1990s and found themselves retrenching and consolidating.

Fortunately for entrepreneurs, though, new resources have moved in to pick up some of the slack. They include major corporations, foreign investors, and brokerage firms. By the middle of 1991, *The Economist* ran an editorial that observed, "The banks no longer dominate the financial system. Deregulation has brought in lots of new lenders, and new ways of bringing lenders and borrowers together. By some definitions, banks now account for barely a quarter of all the money advanced to firms and households in America."

Entrepreneurs should always keep in mind — no matter how badly the search for financing may seem to be going — that they are part of a very desirable market from the viewpoint of many large institutions. The institutions are well aware that many of America's most innovative products and services originate with young growing businesses. In many cases, the executives of these institutions want to establish relationships with young businesses in the hopes that these relationships will expand as the businesses grow. Just because you are running into rejection doesn't mean there isn't a financing source out there for you. As Art Snyder of US Trust Corp. suggests at the very beginning of this chapter, you may have to search harder for "the better bank," or other financial backer. In this next section I examine both the old standbys and some of the more recent candidates for financing assistance.

• **Banks: looking for double security.** One of the most common misconceptions entrepreneurs have about banks is that they evaluate businesses in the same way investors do. Entrepreneurs are invariably disappointed when they are rejected for bank loans after having provided bankers with evidence of the growth opportunities their businesses represent.

The fundamental truth that these entrepreneurs overlook is that banks care much less about how well your business will grow than they do about getting their loans repaid. As a consequence, bankers are most concerned with two primary issues when they evaluate a young business for a loan: First, does the business have the cash flow to make the required loan payments? Second, if the business should run into hard times and have insufficient cash flow to keep up with the loan payments, does it have collateral in the form of machinery, real estate, inventory, or other items that will provide repayment of the loan?

A key challenge for entrepreneurs, then, is to be able to demonstrate that they have both the cash flow and the collateral to ease bankers' understandable concerns. These aren't easy for most new or early-stage businesses to demonstrate. Service businesses, in particular, tend to have little in the way of the machinery, inventory, and real estate that banks desire as collateral.

Even if they do manage to meet the two basic criteria, entrepreneurs face additional uncertainty, thanks to upheavals in the banking industry that struck in the late 1980s and early 1990s. As I noted earlier, banks have become a less important source of financing because many got into trouble by making too many risky real estate loans. In an effort to bail themselves out of those loans as the real estate market deteriorated, the banks in many cases did two things: They demanded early repayment of loans from companies that were current on outstanding loans, and they avoided making new loans to smaller companies. The bottom line was that young businesses — even those that met the two main criteria I described — encountered difficulties getting bank loans.

As the banking climate improves, entrepreneurs should keep in mind the lessons of the late 1980s and early 1990s, says Art Snyder, a vice chairman of US Trust Corp., a holding company of banks in the Northeast. He offers the following advice:

Deal only with stable banks. "Always go to a good bank. Never go to a troubled bank. Be careful of the troubled banks, because when they get further into trouble, they will call the good loans before they call the bad ones because they need liquidity . . . .You want to know what the bank's reputation is when it rains. Will the bank give you the umbrella or will it run for cover?"

Get an introduction. "Go to your suppliers or the people you sell to and ask them who they bank with. What's your relationship?. . .Will you introduce me to your banker?"

Start as high up as possible. Snyder advises finding the senior loan officer and asking to be put in touch with the best loan officer on his or her staff. That way, you will get an expert appraisal and a fair hearing.

Emphasize your interest in a long-term relationship. "Tell the banker how you think it is a good bank and why you picked it and how you chose that bank officer specifically and how you went over with the senior loan officer how good that bank officer is. Then you will be surprised at how that bank officer is interested in your little company. Then you can tell him about how good your little company is."

Be careful about what you are pledging. Snyder doesn't make this point, but I believe entrepreneurs should not lose sight of the risks involved with bank loans. Banks will almost always require the owners to sign personal guarantees for company loans. This means that if the business fails and the company's collateral isn't sufficient to repay the principal, the banks can come after the owners' personal property. And don't think they won't do it. I know of several entrepreneurs who lost their homes and other property to banks seeking to recover payments due on business loans. This isn't to say an entrepreneur should never personally sign for a loan. Just know what you are getting yourself into.

- **Venture capitalists: less venturesome.** Probably the key fact for entrepreneurs to remember about venture capital firms is that their names are misleading. Though the term *venture capital* suggests a willingness to take risks on young companies, the fact is *venture capital* firms have become much less venturesome. More and more have shied away from funding start-up companies and have moved instead to target more established businesses.

    And even if you manage to attract their attention, you will quickly discover why they are often referred to derisively by some entrepreneurs as "vulture capitalists." They drive a hard bargain, seeking as much as 70% of a company in exchange for their investment.

    One encouraging development among venture capital firms, though, has been their growing willingness to look beyond their traditional turf of high technology and become involved with consumer products, retailing, manufacturing, and service companies. This has broadened the possibilities for nontechnology companies.

    Venture capital firms have also shown increasing flexibility in the kinds of arrangements they will negotiate. Whereas they traditionally took equity for their investment, some now make part of their funds available as loans, perhaps convertible into stock some years later.

    As you consider approaching venture capitalists, keep in mind the following observations of Jeffry Timmons, a professor of entrepreneurship at Harvard Business School, who has extensively researched the venture capital industry:

    Tough odds. "The reality of venture capital is that it is a very specialized, very focused activity in this country and it is not for everybody. Out of 100 proposals for start-up companies or expanding small companies the venture capital investors get in this country every year, they will only make an investment in one, two, sometimes three of those 100 proposals. So the real odds of raising money are very slim for most entrepreneurs."

Management focus. "In real estate you hear the saying all the time that the key is location, location, location. For venture capitalists, the thing that they are looking to more than anything else is management, management, management and, lastly, the market potential. What is the quality of the entrepreneur and the people who are trying to get this venture off the ground and grow it? Do they have the experience, the know-how, the commitment, and the real determination and ability to see this thing through and bring it to fruition?"

Grand plans. Venture capitalists are only interested in small companies that have big potential, real big potential. After management qualities, says Timmons, the venture capitalists look at market opportunity. "The ideal deal that the venture capital people are looking for... is a $50-million to $100-million company in sales in five years. It should be in a marketplace that might be $300 million, $400 million, or $500 million in sales at that point in time, with the potential of being a billion-dollar industry in this country. Think of things like microcomputer software, fiber optics, telecommunications."

Value added. If you do get venture capitalists interested in your company and are able to negotiate what you consider reasonable terms, your company may gain from their experience, says Timmons. Having venture capitalists involved in your company, whether on its board of directors or as advisers, "is a tremendous advantage and a tremendously valuable secret weapon in your effort to grow a substantial high-performing company." They can provide suggestions and advice, contacts with other financing sources, and contacts with potential customers.

• *The federal government: depending on banks.* Back in the early 1980s, the federal government, via the U.S. Small Business Administration, made hundreds of millions of dollars of direct loans annually to small businesses unable to obtain bank financing. It's still possible to obtain up to $750,000 in individual company loans via the SBA, but it's much tougher because the money being made available is bank funds — guaranteed up to 90% by the SBA. The fact that the SBA guarantees repayment of most of the loan makes it more attractive to a bank than a conventional bank loan. But many banks have been reluctant to get involved because of fear of the government bureaucracy and SBA limitations on the interest rates that can be charged.

In an effort to make money more available to early-stage businesses, the agency in the early 1990s started a Small Loan Program, in which entrepreneurs could apply to banks and other lenders for loans of up to $50,000. In an effort to encourage banks to participate more fully, the SBA allowed the banks to charge slightly higher interest rates than before. For information on this and other SBA loan programs, contact your local SBA office or the agency's Small Business Answer Desk at (800) U-ASK-SBA.

- *Corporations: seeking strategic alliances.* Helping make up for the slack in bank lending and venture capital investing, many large corporations during the late 1980s and early 1990s began aggressively pursuing relationships with innovative start-up and early-stage businesses. This trend grew out of the realization by the corporations that in trying to compete in the new global economy, it was no longer possible or even preferable for one company to be able to do all the new-product development, marketing, and other tasks necessary to stay ahead of competitors. So companies ranging from DuPont to IBM to Digital Equipment to AT&T to American Express began cutting deals with tiny companies to engage in joint development, joint distribution, and other joint efforts involving new products and services.

These deals can take any number of forms. In some cases, the corporation provides a research grant in exchange for exclusive licensing rights to the new product. Another option is the corporation buys stock in the small company and the partners work jointly to develop new products. Or the corporation sells a small company's product under the corporate name and pays a percentage of sales to the small company. Sometimes the partnerships involve several large and small companies or even a federal government laboratory. The assistance provided by the corporation may include access to its research facilities or use of its distribution network rather than just cash. Clearly, there are infinite numbers of possible arrangements and terms.

The downside of strategic alliances is that they may limit a small company's options down the road. If you grant a corporation exclusive rights to sell your product in exchange for R&D funds, you may regret the decision if the corporation does a poor job of selling the product, and other marketing opportunities become apparent to you.

Entrepreneurs interested in pursuing strategic alliances need to learn — through their industry associations, suppliers, customers, and other contacts — about the best candidates. Then, just as in the case of banks, the entrepreneurs need to determine who in the corporation has responsibility and authority for pursuing a possible arrangement. Clearly, though, strategic alliances hold out the promise of becoming an increasingly important form of financial support for early-stage companies.

- *Foreign investors: in search of the leading edge.* For all the talk about America losing in competition with foreign companies, the fact remains that foreigners look favorably on the United States as a place to invest — especially in new and growing companies. Foreign companies and investors are especially intrigued with new technology being developed in the States.

  Foreign investment is a form of venture capital, though often at much more favorable terms. Because foreign companies can actually market the products developed by U.S. companies, the foreigners can afford to take a smaller amount of stock in a young company than venture capitalists, figuring that future sales and profits will be part of the return on the investment.

How does an entrepreneur go about finding potential foreign investors? From my experience, accountants with the largest firms seem to have the best contacts with foreigners. It may also be possible to meet them at industry trade shows, both here and overseas. It happens via networking, pure and simple.

- *Nonbank lending: muscling into the small-business market.* While banks were preoccupied with their problems with bad real estate loans among other issues, nonbank lenders have tried to fill at least

A GLANCE AT THE FINANCING SOURCES

SOURCE	Loan or Investment	Financial Risk	Emotional Risk	Amount Available	Difficulty of Obtaining
Personal funds	Investment	High	Uncertain	Variable	Little
Personal borrowing	Loan	High	Low	Up to value per assets	Medium
Family/ Friends	Both	Low	High	Variable	Little
Angels	Both	Low	Low	Up to $1 million	High
Banks	Loan	High	Low	Variable	High
Venture capital	Investment primarily	Low	Low	$500K to $10 million	High
SBA	Loan	High	Low	$750K max	Medium
Strategic alliances	Investment primarily	Low	Low	Variable	High
Foreign investment	Investment	Low	Low	Variable	High
Nonbank loans	Loan	High	Low	Up to $10 million	High
Franchising	Investment	Low	Medium	Variable	Medium

some of the void. These include loan companies, asset-based lenders, and brokerage firms. Like banks, these firms are primarily interested in making sure that small-company borrowers have both the cash flow and the collateral to cover the loan. Unlike banks, they have been more flexible, sometimes in return for higher interest rates than banks might charge.

It's very difficult for start-up companies to qualify for loans from these sources. And because these lenders tend to require personal guarantees, it's important to go into any such loan arrangements with your eyes wide open.

- *Franchising: a pyramid approach.* For young companies in need of expansion capital, franchising can be surprisingly effective. Essentially, a small company sells its name and formula for success to other entrepreneurs, or franchisees, who open outlets under the company banner. The franchiser receives up-front fees and ongoing royalties based on franchisee sales. In effect, the franchisees finance fast growth.

  Clearly, the product or service best suited for franchising is one that can be easily duplicated by others. Fast-food hamburgers and pizza are the classic examples, but in recent years everything from haircutting salons to storefront mailbox rentals have been franchised.

  The circumstances under which companies franchise their products or services have also changed over the years. It used to be that a company had to have a substantial number of company outlets before it was considered a suitable franchise candidate. Some franchisers, though, have taken to starting one or two outlets to prove the franchising potential of a product or service and then selling franchises.

  Before trying to franchise your company's product or service, keep a few points in mind. First, while a company can expand quickly by franchising, total revenues will be lower than they would be with company-owned outlets. Second, selling franchises is a marketing task with special requirements, and you will likely want to engage the services of a consultant or firm that specializes in the task. Third, you will need to find legal assistance to ensure you comply with federal and state disclosure regulations before offering franchises for sale.

■ Getting the Financing You Need

As a start-up entrepreneur, it should be clear by this point that there are many options for financing. Each has its advantages and risks. Here are some overall guidelines to keep in mind as you try to decide which to pursue:

* **Start with close-to-home sources.** These are easier for a start-up entrepreneur to obtain than institutional sources. Once you obtain such financing, you can use it as leverage to improve your chances for institutional financing.

* **Understand all the potential costs.** As should be apparent from the descriptions of financing sources, each has its special costs, not only financially but emotionally. Hitting a business slump can cost you dearly if you are unable to keep up with loan payments — to the extent of losing personal property. Obtaining money from relatives and friends can have long-term emotional fallout.

* **Be businesslike.** No matter what the source — and this includes parents, in-laws, and friends — be as open and straightforward as possible. Put together written agreements and stick to them. When approaching institutional sources, you should similarly be open about your past successes and previous problems, such as with credit or being fired from a previous job. Expect that any bank or other institutional source will investigate you carefully before granting funds and will find any skeletons in your closet. If you tell bankers first, they'll probably admire your honesty. If

they find out in a credit or reference check, they'll figure you were covering up and avoid dealing with you.

- **Try to diversify.** Seek to obtain more than one type and source of financing. That is, you don't want to have too much debt or too much equity. Try not to have your father provide all your financing, even if he is willing and able to commit the whole thing. You want to avoid dependency on one source, just as you want to avoid dependency on one customer or one supplier.

- **Be patient.** It nearly always takes longer than you expect to obtain financing, no matter who you are dealing with.

- **Be prepared with a business plan.** Virtually all institutional sources and even some close-to-home sources require a written business plan before extending funding to new and young businesses. Guidance on putting together a written business plan is the subject of the next chapter.

■ Exercise I: Assessing Your Resources

Here is a list of the potential financing resources considered in this chapter. Next to each one do the following:

1. Rank it terms of its preference to you as a potential source, rating it high, medium, or low.

2. For each source rated as a high preference, list three potential candidates you might approach for financing and the maximum amount you could reasonably expect from each.

3. For each source rated as a medium preference, list two potential candidates you might approach for financing and the maximum amount you could reasonably expect from each.

- Personal funds

- Mortgage of house and other assets.

- Credit cards

- Personal bank loan

- Family/friends

- Angels

- Banks

- Venture capitalists

- Small Business Administration

- Strategic alliances

- Foreign investment

- Nonbank loans

- Franchising

■ Exercise II: Analyzing Your Best Sources

Make some determinations about your highest-preference sources:

1. How much can you reasonably expect to raise from these sources?

2. How does this amount compare with the amount you determined from your cash-flow analysis in Chapter 6 is necessary to start your business?

3. If it is less than what you think you require, what can you do to reduce the amount you'll need or increase the amount you can obtain?

THE BEST BUSINESS PLAN FOR YOU

"If you don't have that road map, you really are putting yourself at a serious disadvantage."

....

James A. Lowry, James A. Lowry Associates

Business planning tends to get treated as an academic exercise by many writers and consultants. They talk about such things as "the planning process," "deriving a strategy," "the organizational hierarchy," and "modeling approaches."

Before you begin yawning, let me say that I don't view planning as an academic exercise. I view it as a much more active and exciting part of the entire business process.

At the end of the previous chapter, I pointed out that a prerequisite for approaching financing sources is having a written business plan. Never has that been more true than it is in the 1990s. Indeed, for many entrepreneurs, writing a business plan is synonymous with raising money — it's a chore you do to have a shot at the cash.

As Frank Carney, the founder of Pizza Hut, points out: "We got our financing from our mother. She didn't require us to submit a plan. If that would have been one person removed from [their mother], and would have been a next-door neighbor, you bet we would have had to take something [written]. . . to get $300 each."

But the business plan shouldn't be viewed as merely a means to raise money. Certainly a business plan is essential for approaching many financing sources. It needs to be viewed in a larger context, however. My feeling is that it will only be successful in helping you raise money if you have dealt with it in this larger context.

This chapter deals with the most important issues raised in the planning process, so you can begin work on a business plan that will have the maximum effectiveness possible for your new company.

■ What Is a Business Plan?

As basic as this question may seem, it is the most appropriate place to begin the planning process. Having the right view of the business plan will help you develop the kind of plan that will do you and your business the most good.

All kinds of definitions are thrown around about what a business plan is. The "road map" metaphor used by James Lowry at the start of this chapter is a common, appropriate one. Others take account of tactics and strategy.

I like to offer two possible definitions of a business plan, partly for the sake of contrast. Both are accurate but, as you may conclude, one definition is perhaps more dynamic and useful in setting the business plan's direction and tone.

Definition 1:
A business plan is a document that convincingly demonstrates that your business can sell enough of its product or service to make a satisfactory profit and be attractive to potential backers.

Definition 2:
A business plan is a selling document. It sells your business and its executives to potential backers of your business, from bankers

to investors to partners to employees.

As you may have guessed, I prefer the second definition. At its most fundamental level, a business plan should be a selling document. It should sell the business to those I refer to as stakeholders. There are many potential stakeholders, as I discuss in the next section.

Whichever definition you prefer, be aware that a business plan isn't a document that you sit down and write over a weekend. Invariably, it is the result of many weeks and months of research and evaluation.

Many entrepreneurs agonize about writing a business plan because they find it so difficult to get started. As you go through the start-up process of evaluating ideas, considering prospective employees, and calculating cash-flow needs, you should take notes and answer the questions posed in the exercises in this book. When you do those things, you find that nearly without realizing it, you have begun writing. This chapter provides additional matters for you to deal with in your writing efforts. Before too long, you are on your way to having a business plan.

■ Why Write a Business Plan?

Every entrepreneur has a business plan. The problem is that more often than not, it is in his or her head and is not written down. It was that way for Gordon Segal when he started Crate & Barrel. "We didn't have any strategic plan. When you open a small business, the strategic plan is in your head."

The problem is, a plan that is in your head is a lot different from one that is written down. It is less precise. It is more fluid. It is unknown to others working with you. Mo Siegel of Celestial Seasonings puts the difficulty this way: "If you don't want very many vacations and you want to work late at night, just wing it and you will be winging it constantly. You will be fighting fires all the time."

The differences between a mental plan and a written plan help explain why transferring the plan from your head to paper is very challenging. If you talk to entrepreneurs who have gone through the process of writing a complete business plan, you invariably learn that it was one of the most difficult tasks they ever accomplished. Which is understandable, when you stop to think about it. Few of us really enjoy exerting the discipline required to turn into writing something as demanding and complex as the workings of a business.

The upshot is that you ought to have some compelling reasons for writing a business plan before you begin such an arduous task. It turns out that there are many extremely important reasons for writing a business plan. Here are seven of the most important:

1. **To sell yourself on the business.** If you've done all the things I've suggested up until now, you are probably close to being ready to start your company. You've come up with a solid idea, considered people to hire, evaluated your cash requirements, and begun getting financing together.

   But are you really *sold* on starting this business? After all, once you actually begin operations, there will be no turning back. It will be an all-consuming job with high stakes. Is it possible you want to stay at your current job or find another job instead? Would you be better off considering a different business to start?

   David Liederman points out that he spent two years researching and planning his cookie retail business from the time that he actually found "religion" in the Berkeley cookie store (as quoted at the start of Chapter 1).

   When Fred Gibbons, the founder of Software Publishing, a maker of personal computer software, was considering starting his company back in 1980, he was a rising star at Hewlett-Packard. To start the business, he was about to take out a $50,000 second mortgage on his house. He decided he needed to put his plans down on paper to serve as a sanity check to determine if he was doing the right thing.

167

When you put your plan on paper, you discover questions and issues that may not have been apparent when you were mulling the matter in your head. Your ability to deal with those questions and issues are key to helping you decide whether to start the business and if so in what form.

It may be said that writing a business plan poses a psychological risk of sorts, in that you may discover more uncertainties and problems than you originally realized — to the point that you reconsider starting the business. If you become so emotionally intent on starting a business, though, such a prospect will not be very appealing. My feeling is that if the process of planning sells you on holding off and doing something else, it may have saved you considerable anguish — and money.

2. Obtain bank financing. Until the start of the 1990s, a written business plan was an option request by most bankers. All that changed when many banks got themselves in trouble with bad real estate loans. Suddenly, federal bank regulators were looking over their shoulders ever more intensely. And because banks cut back on their lending in many cases, the competition for small-business loans intensified greatly. In addition to simply filling out a bank form about your credit references and personal assets, you are now expected to provide a written business plan to be considered for a loan by most banks.

According to Art Snyder of US Trust Corp., "I like to see a document saying who the people are, who the head of the company is. . . . I would like to know what the manufacturing plant looks like, what the rent is, what the overhead costs are, what the fixed liabilities are down the street. . . . I want him to tell me how big the marketplace is, who else is in the marketplace, and how it is structured. He should be able to tell me how he is going to reach the marketplace — through dealers, distributors, direct mail, direct salesmen, reps, and how he is going to pay those people. He should be able to explain his gross margins." All the issues Snyder alludes to should be covered in a business plan, and they are dealt with later in this chapter.

3. Seek investment funds. For established venture capital firms, a written business plan is a ticket of admission to any kind of serious discussions. And even so-called angels increasingly ask for business plans from entrepreneurs seeking funds. As Frank Carney pointed out earlier in this chapter, he would have expected just about any investor, except his mother, to require his business plan. Thinking about it from an angel's viewpoint, you wouldn't be too impressed if an entrepreneur approached you for funds and when asked for a business plan, you got a blank stare or a mumbled, "We're just getting to that."

4. Arrange strategic alliances. If you are considering approaching a corporation about entering into a strategic alliance, don't expect to get very far without a written plan. Chances are that several corporate officials, perhaps from different groups or departments, will review the possibility of becoming involved with your company. There is no way they can reasonably expect to evaluate the appropriateness of your company without a written business plan.

5. Obtain large contracts. Young companies sometimes find themselves in a position to make a large sale to an established company — even a major corporation. In that situation, though, the customer will undoubtedly be concerned about other issues beyond your ability to simply deliver what you say you will deliver. The company may be concerned about subsequent service if your product is flawed. The company may also worry about getting spare parts when the product needs maintenance. And the company may wonder about getting consistent product or service quality over a period of several years.

So the larger company may come back to you and say, "Lots

of people know who we are, but no one knows who you are. How can we be sure you'll be around next year or even next month to follow up on what you've sold us?"

At that point, it's nice to be able to pull out a copy of your business plan and invite the potential buyer to take a look. The business plan demonstrates that you've thought well beyond next week and next month — that you are thinking ahead several years and have plans for what you will accomplish.

6. Attract key employees. When a new or early-stage company goes to hire top managers, it faces a quandary not unlike that described in the previous section about selling to large companies. A prospective manager your company wants to hire may be considering leaving a secure job with a larger business and wondering how long your company is going to be around. If he or she gets too insecure, you may not convince that person to join your company.

Once again, a business plan serves an important purpose in reassuring the prospect that you are thinking ahead and have specific plans for the future. In the case of recruiting, it can also save you much valuable time explaining all your plans and answering the many questions a prospective manager is likely to ask.

7. Complete mergers and acquisitions. Once your company becomes more established, you may want to consider either acquiring another company or making your company available for acquisition. In either case, a business plan can make you a more attractive candidate. In either situation, you can expect there will be more companies in the chase than just yours.

If you want to make an acquisition, the company you want to acquire may have several other suitors. Assuming the owner wants to stay on after the merger or the price being paid is dependent on the acquired company's future earnings, he or she will likely be careful about who gets the company. (And you may want to be sure that any company you acquire has its own business plan.)

Similarly, if you want to sell your company, you can expect that potential buyers are looking at lots of other companies besides yours. So it will be important to stand out from the crowd.

A business plan can help you accomplish your goals by presenting you as the owner of a serious business that looks and plans ahead. And as in the previous situation of searching for a key employee, a business plan can save time exchanging information.

■ What Should the Business Plan Cover?

OK, you say, you're convinced. Now how do you go about organizing the plan?

Before I list the areas to be covered, I should point out that each business plan is unique, because each business is unique. So my suggestions for organizing the plan aren't cast in stone; you may want to make alterations to suit the specifics of your business.

My feeling about the uniqueness of businesses has broader ramifications. It means that I am not enthusiastic about software programs that allow entrepreneurs to fill in the blanks to create a business plan. The underlying assumption of those programs is that all businesses are basically alike and that it's only the details of markets, production, management, and finance that distinguish them.

With those disclaimers, here is a brief overview of the contents of the written plan:

- **Cover Page.** Here you provide the name of your company, its address and phone number, and the founder's/chief executive's name. As obvious as that may seem, many entrepreneurs inadvertently fail to include such basic information. As a consequence, when a banker, investor, or other stakeholder becomes interested in your business, he or she has to scrounge for a phone book or call directory assistance to contact you. Suddenly, you've frustrated and perhaps irritated someone whose allegiance you are trying to win — not a smart way to do business.

And if the plan is going to be distributed to several bankers or investors, make sure you number each plan prominently on the cover page and include a statement to the effect that the document contains proprietary material and shouldn't be photocopied. These steps enable you to keep track of who has your plans and hopefully deters recipients from copying or widely circulating the plan. (You may also want recipients to sign a nondisclosure statement, which is best drawn up with assistance from an attorney.)

- **Table of Contents.** This should include a logical listing of all the business plan's sections, together with section and page numbers. This also seems obvious, but lots of business plans I have seen either contain no contents page or, if they do, they leave off page numbers. I list a sample table of contents (see page 173), but you may need to add special sections to take account of your industry. For example, if you are planning to manufacture toys, you may need a special section addressing the issue of product liability and insurance.

- **Executive Summary.** This is the single most important section of the business plan. That's because most readers — especially lenders and investors — turn to it first and decide, based on the three or four minutes they spend skimming it, whether to take the rest of the plan seriously.

   Before I explain what an executive summary is, I need to explain what it *isn't*. It isn't an abstract, an introduction, a preface, or a random collection of highlights. Rather, an executive summary is *the business plan in miniature*. As such, it should be able to stand alone as a kind of business plan within the business plan. It should be logical, clear, interesting — and exciting. It should sell your business.

SAMPLE TABLE OF CONTENTS

YOUR COMPANY'S BUSINESS PLAN

- Executive Summary
- The Company
- The Market
- The Product or Service
- Sales and Promotion
- Manufacturing (if necessary)
- Financial Data
- Appendices

The executive summary succeeds by capturing readers' attention and imaginations, enticing them to read more and conveying the flavor of the rest of the plan. When readers finish the executive summary, they should have a good sense of what you are trying to do in your business. They should also be enthused enough to read on and learn more about your company.

The executive summary should be no longer than two typewritten pages. If capturing an entire business plan within two pages sounds like a difficult task, it is. I suggest that entrepreneurs begin the process of putting together their business plans by writing a draft of the executive summary, then putting together the full plan, and finally revising the executive summary when everything else has been completed.

- **The Company.** The section after the executive summary is where you articulate your company's underlying philosophy and logic. You do that by covering two basic subjects: your company's strategy and its management team.

  Strategy. This is really a fancy term for your company's overall approach to producing and selling its products and/or services. You should have certain underlying principles and approaches to doing business that enable you to build on your strengths and distinguish your company from the competition.

It could be that your focus on product quality and low-cost supply sources — as in the case of Crate & Barrel — enables your business to achieve a competitive advantage. Or your focus on developing proprietary technology may allow you to build a product line with price and profit margin advantages to gain a niche in the marketplace.

One approach to describing your strategy in an understandable and convincing way is to break this section down into three parts — past, present, and future. Thus, under the title of "Background," you explain the company's origin and development. When was the company founded and what was its original strategy? How has the strategy changed in the face of market research and initial sales efforts?

A section on "Current Status" examines the company today in terms of its strengths and weaknesses. The latter need not be of the company-threatening sort; it may be you don't have as much production space as you would like or you are unable to expand capacity. These can be cast in terms of opportunities that can be most effectively exploited with financing.

Most important is the section looking toward the future, usually called "Objectives." Based on the company's history and experience to date, you set sales, profit, production, quality, and other objectives — your means of achieving success. For a start-up company that by its very nature has little history or current experience, you have to base your objectives on your assessment of the marketplace, your resources, and your sense of what can be accomplished. The more data you can back it up with, the better.

Management Team. With matters of strategy dealt with, you can move on to the management team. As Jeffry Timmons noted in the previous chapter, it's people who venture capitalists (and other investors and lenders) are most concerned about. For a start-up especially, potential stakeholders will search in your business plan for clues as to whether the people involved in your company are up to the task. These stakeholders will want to know that there is a team involved and that they have achieved previous business success. Investors and lenders feel most comfortable with a team managing a company rather than a single individual. They also prefer to see people who have successfully gone through the start-up process before — and have complementary skills (rather than all being engineers or from a sales background). Your business plan should devote about one-third to one-half page describing each of the key management team members.

- **The Market.** Who are your customers? Describing the market involves identifying your customer prospects and determining how best to reach them. It should be noted, however, that marketing is *not* the same thing as selling or promoting; they are separate tasks. Selling and promoting are the implementation of your marketing plan.

    Before you can answer who your customers are, you must determine exactly what your company is selling — not in terms of product or service features but in terms of what benefits customers are gaining. Does the product or service you sell help people save money or make money? Does it make them feel better? Does it provide convenience or improve productivity? Once you've identified customer benefits, you are in a good position to describe those who will most want what your company is selling.

    The next step is to provide evidence that enough customers exist to make your product/service profitable. That evidence must come from market analysis that identifies precisely who your customer prospects are (all the residents of your town, just those under age 25, those over age 65, or only women, etc.). You'll want to say whether the market is growing or shrinking and, finally, whether there are enough potential customers to justify the business you are establishing. You may find you have a tremendous product or service that some group of prospective customers loves and is willing to pay for — only to discover that there aren't enough of them to allow you to build a profitable business. David Liederman had something of that problem with his gourmet-sauce business; because not enough individuals really understood what he was selling, he was going after too small a market of knowledgeable customers.

The basis of your answers comes from market research — Census data, market studies, news articles. And the answers must be cast in terms of the competition. How will your company's product or service satisfy customers better than what is already in the marketplace?

This should be the longest single section of the business plan — probably twice as long as the section that follows.

- **The Product/Service.** Here is where you do what most entrepreneurs like to do best: describe the features of your product or service. Indeed, many entrepreneurs become so enamored of their product or service that they make light of market issues. They figure their product or service is so wonderful, how could people not want to buy it?

But your product or service features should be described in terms of what the market prefers. It could be that as much as you would like to make landscape design a part of your lawn service, that you shouldn't because the middle-class area in which you are operating prefers basic lawn-and-hedge-trimming services. You may even scare some prospects off if you offer a fancy-sounding service like landscape design, because they'll figure you are too expensive.

You must also take into account whether you can deliver the product or service you promise on time and with the quality the market demands. More than one company — particularly in the computer software field — has gotten itself in trouble by announcing a new product and then failing to come through at the promised date, or by delivering a product that was seriously flawed.

Finally and perhaps most important, can you deliver what

you have promised and still make a profit? In the section on cash flow, James Lowry alluded to the fact that his consulting firm, in its eagerness to attract clients, wound up promising more than it should have at the agreed-on prices. There are few things worse than having to tell customers that the price you quoted or advertised isn't the real price because higher-than-expected costs forced a hike. You can expect little sympathy; indeed, there's a likelihood you will lose customers who either don't feel the new price is justified or are simply irritated with your unbusinesslike approach.

- *Sales and Promotion.* Now that you've identified your prospective customers and the product or service you will provide, you need to determine how you will reach your customers and sell to them. Do you have an in-house sales force, or will you use manufacturer's representatives, direct mail, or contracted telemarketers to sell your product/service? Do you expect to do advertising to let prospective customers know about your product, or will you rely on public relations?

  Along with determining the best way to sell and promote your product or service, you must determine if your approach is the most cost-effective one. If you are manufacturing specialized clothing and would like to have your own sales force selling it, you may discover that the price at which most buyers would still buy isn't high enough to support the salespeople's salaries and commissions. So it may be necessary to rely on manufacturer's reps, who can divide the costs of handling your line of clothing with those of other noncompeting lines. As a general guideline, the costs associated with selling should not be more than 10% of revenues.

  You will almost certainly discover that you can't afford the kind of advertising or public relations program you would like to do. Think of ways to be creative, such as doing some of your own public relations by getting to know editors of publications that reach your market, writing an article for them, or providing them with news that would incorporate mention of your product or service.

- **Manufacturing.** This section is only necessary, of course, if your company is making a product. It should discuss your supply sources, equipment, capacity, and quality control. If you are subcontracting certain components or processes, the subcontractors' capacities should be discussed. Can the subcontractors deliver on time? This section should also provide information about manufacturing costs.

- **Finances.** The business plan needs to provide as clear and precise a picture as possible of your company's financial condition. You provide that picture primarily through a presentation of three types of financial statements: cash flow, income statement, and balance sheet. Your business plan should discuss the most important revelations and issues raised by the financial statements, such as when your business will reach break-even, when it is expected to become profitable, and what the most significant expenses are. Based on the statements, this section should also say something about the company's financial requirements over the coming five years; if you are using the business plan to seek a loan or investment, you should state how much you need and the form in which you prefer it (loan, sale of stock, combination debt and equity, etc.).

These statements should go back as long as you have been in business (up to five years) and, in the cases of the cash-flow and income statements, should also project three to five years in the future. Now you may be saying, how can I project ahead three to five years when I don't know what tomorrow brings? You can't do it with any precision, but you must try anyway. If your company has an operating history, you should be able to use your past performance as guidance in looking ahead. Here is some detail about the three types of financial statements:

Cash flow. I discussed cash flow at length in Chapter 6. For the purpose of your business plan, you should track cash flow historically and on a monthly basis for the first year and quarterly for the next two to four years. The cash-flow statement helps show when and under what circumstances the break-even point will be reached.

Income statement. Sometimes called the profit-and-loss statement or the P&L, the income statement reports the results of your business from an accounting point of view over a specific period of time, typically quarterly or yearly. In addition to being considered essential information by lenders and investors, it is used to calculate your federal and state income taxes and should be prepared by your accountant.

The income statement asks, did we make any money — not in terms of cash but in terms of proper accounting rules? It reports net sales, less costs and expenses to arrive at income or loss before taxes. Generally, sales and expenses are recorded when they occur, not when the cash is actually received or paid out. Therefore, in an income statement, revenues from sales is not the same as revenues from sales in our cash-flow statement. (For a sample income statement, see page 180.)

In your projections, the income statement should look ahead quarterly for the first two years and annually thereafter.

Balance sheet. While not particularly useful for start-up businesses, a balance sheet is required by most lenders and some investors. The balance sheet is a status report. It states the company's financial condition at a specific time — generally year-end. Its left side lists the business's assets — the things it owns. The right side lists equities that are the claims against the assets. There are two categories of equities: liabilities, which are the claims of outsiders such as banks and suppliers, and owners' equity, which are the claims of owners or shareholders. (For a sample balance sheet, see page 181)

The statement is called a balance sheet because the left side, assets, must equal the right side, liabilities plus owners' equity. Why? Because all the assets of a business are claimed either by the outside creditors or by the owners. The worth of the business, the owners' equity, is equal to what it owns (the assets), minus what it owes (the liabilities).

- **Appendix.** Because your business plan should be as concise as possible, there may be certain material you want readers to be aware of that doesn't fit into the body of the plan. Prime among such material would be "love letters" from customers or pros-

SAMPLE INCOME STATEMENT

YOUR COMPANY

GROSS SALES		$3,000
(Less) returns	$100	
Bad debt	$100	
Total	$200	
NET SALES		**$2,800**
(Less) cost of goods sold		
Materials	$1,000	
Shipping	$300	
Total	$1,300	
GROSS PROFIT		**$1,500**
EXPENSES		
Rent	$700	
Payroll	$1,000	
Total	$1,700	
INCOME (LOSS) BEFORE TAXES	($200)	

pects — notes about how great they think your product or service is. Additional material for the appendix may include resumés, product descriptions, and news articles about the company. One approach is simply to lump all such material together in an appendix that readers can review after they've read the plan. Or if such material is too voluminous, you can simply create a second volume that is made available to individuals who want to learn more about your company.

■ How Long Should the Business Plan Be?

There is no right answer to this question. Business plans vary according to the type and complexity of the business, as well as how much history needs to be included. To provide guidance on this issue, I have categorized business plans into three broad types as follows:

SAMPLE BALANCE SHEET

YOUR COMPANY

Current assets		Total current liabilities	$145,000
Cash	$50,000		
Inventory	$60,000		
Total current assets	$110,000	Total liabilities	$145,000
Fixed assets		Owners' equity	
Land	$60,000	Common stock	$105,000
Buildings	$80,000		
Total fixed assets	$140,000	Total owners' equity	$105,000
Total assets	$250,000	Total liabilities & Owners' equity	$250,000

- **Summary business plan.** As the name suggests, this is an abridged business plan that typically runs ten pages or less. It is appropriate for many start-up businesses — especially those seeking bank financing or the backing of friends and relatives. Because a start-up business has little in the way of history (aside from the owners' careers), it is often possible to condense the business plan to such a slim size.

- **Full business plan.** This is the more traditional business plan, usually between ten and forty pages. Such a length allows for full exploration of the key issues. Any business seeking in excess of $500,000 of financing or a strategic partner should expect to do a full business plan.

- **Operational business plan.** This is a plan that an existing company puts together to guide its managers on the company's overall direction and goals. It should be updated annually to allow for changes in the business environment. Because it goes into detail about company operations, it is invariably longer than a summary plan or a full business plan, running in excess of forty pages, sometimes to 100-plus pages.

■ Getting Down to Business

Having provided an overview of the business plan, I know there is no easy way around the rigors of putting together a written plan. But there are ways to make the writing process more efficient and the final product more useful:

- **View the business plan as your company's representative.** Because many readers will be meeting you through the plan, make it reflective of you and your company. View it as your company's representative — almost like a company resumé. That may mean substituting a more conversational tone for stilted language. You may want to include a drawing or photo of your company's product on the title page. You should also tend to details like misspellings and grammatical errors. Feel free to have an English teacher or copy editor look over your plan before finalizing it.

• **Consider customizing your plan for different audiences.** There's nothing written in concrete that a company can have only one business plan. If you will be showing your plan to a variety of financing sources — for instance, bankers, venture capitalists, and corporate representatives — you may want to adjust the plan for each. As I pointed out in the previous chapter, bankers are primarily interested in cash flow and the quality of your company's assets. Venture capitalists look principally at growth prospects. So you could have one plan for the bankers to emphasize the issues that concern them, another for the venture capitalists, and still a third for corporate types. The plans would use much material in common, of course, but key sections could be changed to provide emphasis.

• **Acknowledge weaknesses.** Entrepreneurs are usually reluctant to admit potential weaknesses in their businesses even to themselves, let alone in written form to strangers. But it is essential that the business plan anticipate potential problems and address them candidly. It may be that your company requires regulatory approval — say, from the U.S. Food and Drug Administration for a pharmaceutical product — before marketing can begin. More likely, your company will be starting up in a field that has lots of competition. You need to acknowledge this challenge and name competitors, assess their strengths and weaknesses, and explain how your new company will beat out these competitors.

• **Keep rewriting.** Ask a professional writer what the secret of successful writing is and he or she will most likely tell you, rewriting. Even professionals rarely get it right the first time. Unfortunately, entrepreneurs often become frustrated when their writing is awkward and imprecise in a first draft. It may be necessary to rewrite some parts of the business plan four, five, or six times to get it the way it should be. Moreover, the day the plan is complete, it becomes outmoded. With the pace of business change seemingly accelerating, the frequency with which you should update your business plan should also increase. Conventional wisdom is that the business plan should be updated annually, but it's appropriate to think about more frequent updates — semiannually or even quarterly — to reflect changing conditions.

- **Involve your team.** Assuming you have other people working with you to start the business, get them involved in writing the business plan. You may want to ask each individual to write a section or two based on his or her expertise (the marketing person would write the sections on the market and on sales/promotion, for instance). Or if you feel the plan must come from you as the founder and chief executive, then make sure that members of your team have a chance to review your drafts and provide input. Also, be sure to have your accountant review the section on finances. The more input you get, the more clear and convincing the business plan becomes.

It's often said that many successful businesses have been started without the benefit of a business plan. I am well aware of such situations and am the first to acknowledge that it is possible to succeed without a business plan. But a business plan increases the odds in your favor. And in today's challenging business climate, who would want to fight with that?

■ Exercise I: Setting Up Your Business Plan

1. Which of the three types of business plan (summary plan, full plan, operating plan) is most appropriate for you? Why?

2. Begin mapping a table of contents. Consider what subjects must be covered in your plan. Evaluate the subject areas listed earlier in this chapter and decide how you should cover them in your business plan. Decide whether any particular areas must be added to allow you to discuss the special aspects of your industry.

3. Make notes under each subject of your contents. As you think about the subject area jot down a few notes about issues you want to be sure to cover, such as names of competitors (in the section on marketing) or your arguments for subcontracting the manufacturing (in the section on manufacturing).

4. Write a first draft of the business plan's executive summary. Then identify areas that require more work or research on your part as well as areas that you are ready to complete for the plan.

■ Exercise II: Testing Your Knowledge

Match each label in Column A with its appropriate definition in Column B.

COLUMN A	COLUMN B
A. The executive summary	a. Explains how you will access the marketplace. Will you advertise, attend trade shows, issue new products?
B. The company	b. Describes your perception of the company. How will business grow and profit?
C. The market	c. Contains the balance sheet, income statement, and cash-flow analysis.
D. The product or service	d. A two-page, succinct explanation of your business and its activities; the business plan in miniature.
E. Selling	e. Includes love letters from potential or existing customers.
F. Manufacturing	f. Describes the core of your business.
G. Financial data	g. Describes your company in terms of the benefits it offers to prospective customers and candidly discusses the competition (the plan's largest section).
H. Appendices	h. Discusses how you will make or assemble your product, including justification of make/buy decisions.

Answers: A-d; B-b; C-g; D-f; E-a; F-h; G-c; H-e

STARTING OUT ON THE RIGHT FOOT

"Be prepared to make the business the primary relationship in your life."

. . . .

Christine Martindale, founder of Esprit Miami

If you have followed this book's chapters step by step, you have by now accomplished a great deal — tested and refined your idea, attracted the right people, figured out which corporate structure makes the most sense, worked out your cash flow, determined where your money will come from, and put together a business plan.

Everything is ready. All systems are go. You are poised for the launch. What should you do to ensure that you start on the right foot?

Based on my observations of and discussions with many successful entrepreneurs, I believe it is important to have a dual focus at this point — on both mental and business considerations. This chapter is divided that way.

■ Mental Preparation

It's often said by professional athletes that their success is as much mentally as physically based. Of course, they need the physical attributes, but we all know of highly touted athletes who never quite made it for one reason or another — drugs, alcohol, an inability to get along with the coach, prolonged slumps. Whatever the stated reason, the true reason invariably boils down to an inability to overcome the significant mental hurdles on the way to success.

The same thing applies to entrepreneurs. Certainly it's important to have the right business skills and to do all the business preparations discussed previously, but it's also essential to have the right mental attitude to handle the inevitable hurdles, disappointments, and stresses that come with the business start-up territory.

Here are some suggestions from the entrepreneurs we interviewed:

• **Be ready to make a total commitment.** Christine Martindale of Esprit Miami wasn't being facetious when she made the statement at the start of this chapter. She observes: "You have to give up just about everything else in your life. You have to give up your time to the business. You don't say, 'Well, I want to be alone today and take a day off.' You can't take a day off, especially if there are only two people there. You can't take vacations, because if you are not there, the work doesn't get done. If you are successful, then you are getting more and more work. I think you have to count on working twelve hours a day, seven days a week, for at least the first three years you are in business."

That means you need the support of those around you. And even those around you may not realize the extent of the commitment. Frank Carney, a founder of Pizza Hut says: "I can't say that it cost me my first marriage definitely, but it was a heavy contributor, and I know of a lot of people who have gone through the same thing—a very troubled home life, personal life. Being an entrepreneur… causes a demand that makes other things be put on a back burner, and sometimes people can't manage the back burner."

• **Be prepared to sell yourself.** No matter what your product or service, prospective customers will decide whether or not to buy from your start-up business based in large measure on what they think of you. According to James Lowry of James Lowry Associates, "Unless you can sell yourself, unless you are believable to a client or a customer, they are not going to buy it. They have to believe in you. They have to believe in whatever you are selling, that it's going to work. Or else they won't take out the checkbook and write you a check."

Lowry knows well about the need to sell yourself: "When I first started, I had to sell myself because I didn't have anything else. I didn't have any clients. I didn't have any product. I didn't have any track record. So I sold myself. I said, 'Look, I can help you. I can solve your problems. I can make more money for you.' And then with time, I sold the company and sold all the great things we had done with other companies, and we just stayed on that road."

- **Be single-minded in going after those first customers.** Returning to a sports analogy, it's often said in professional baseball that a rookie's first hit is the most difficult one to get, because of all the pressure. The same thing often applies to entrepreneurs — the first sales are the toughest. You face the challenge of getting someone to be the first to go with an unknown quantity.

This is especially true if you are selling a high-ticket product (although it applies to some lower-cost items like a food product, which requires a distributor or retailer to buy in quantity and commit to it for some months). George Kachajian of Silicon Technology vividly recalls his challenge in selling some of his company's first $20,000-plus silicon-slicing machines: "You have to believe in the product you are making and know that the person you are trying to sell to has a reluctance to buy. He doesn't know how great your product is. You are just another person trying to sell something and you have to give that extra flourish, or you have to learn how to give that buyer comfort. That can happen in many different ways. One way it worked for me was that we had a potential buyer in Massachusetts — a woman I had known from my corporate days — who was interested in six or eight machines but was kind of reluctant to place an order with a new company. Will he be in business five years from now? Will he be able to get spare parts? And so on. She gave me the order when I told her we would paint the machines blue — the color of her eyes. She cut the order right there. Eight times $21,000 is a lot of money. To this day, we have the same blue machine as our standard product."

As unusual as that sounds, the larger point is that orders can ride on seemingly small or subjective matters. Being able to determine what makes a prospect tick — and satisfy his or her emotional as well as practical needs — can lead to substantial sales.

■ Business Preparation

Assuming you enter business with the right mental attitude and preparation, the rest of your prep work is really a matter of common sense. Some of this common sense doesn't become apparent until after you've made what in retrospect you realize to be silly mistakes. The entrepreneurs we interviewed provide some practical tips for heading off some of these mistakes.

• *Keep the business simple.* There's an inclination among start-up entrepreneurs to produce a lot more products and provide a lot more services than they should. This inclination stems from two factors: a desire to act on the suggestions entrepreneurs receive from prospective or actual customers along with their own boundless enthusiasm.

The problem with quickly trying to come up with a wide variety of products and services is that you run the risk of diluting your company's overall effectiveness. Rather than doing one or two things really well, you may wind up doing five or six things reasonably well — if you're lucky. More likely, some of your products or services will be of poor quality or poorly timed.

Frank Carney explains the challenge as follows: "Keeping things simple when you first start enables you to do a higher-quality job, and it is really necessary that those very first customers get the highest quality that you can ever produce. What makes a business work in the beginning is word of mouth more than anything else. If you don't do a high-quality job, you don't have positive word of mouth....In our case, we had two sizes of pizza and one basic kind, which was thin pizza, a limited number of drinks, and almost anything that went with the pizza. So we really could concentrate on the pizza the way we were going to make pizza — right every time, or as close to right as we could get. And to me that is simple, if you compare it to what a Pizza Hut is today. They have thin pizza, they have pan pizza, they have sandwiches, they have spaghetti. Those are just some examples of how you can take something simple and make it pretty complex....The lesson there is to keep it as simple as you can when you first start and emphasize the product as the main thing you are selling."

David Liederman of David's Cookies offers similar advice. "You have to be pragmatic," he says. "We started with six cookies and were up to twenty-two by 1986....We've done what McDonald's has done. They started with the hamburger, french fries, milk shake, and soda. Years later, they were up to something like sixty-three products."

So start simple and, if you're successful with a few products or services, *then* add additional ones.

- **Keep a lid on overhead.** It is just as you are preparing to open your business that all kinds of potential new expenses appear. You realize you'll want more space than is afforded by your office at home, and you begin to explore renting an office. Or you decide you really must have a second telephone line. Or you come across what seems like a great deal to purchase a piece of equipment you were planning to rent. Suddenly, your budget of projected expenses is thrown out of whack. I strongly suggest you resist as many of the expense temptations as possible, at least until you have a clear sense of where the business is headed. If business isn't as strong as you had hoped, each dollar you save at the beginning will be available to keep your business alive during the tough times down the road.

- **Be prepared for the unexpected.** There's an old saying in business: "Whatever can go wrong will go wrong." Somehow, it seems to happen in the first few days of many new businesses. You open your restaurant and, at 7:30 p.m., just at the height of the dinner hour, there's a power failure. Or a customer has a heart attack. Or the health inspector arrives with complaints. Or any of a hundred other things go wrong.

  I know of people in the direct-mail business who have brought their first 20,000 or 50,000 promotional letters to the post office for mailing and discovered that the address area or indicia on the envelopes didn't conform to postal regulations. Everything had to be redone at an unbearable cost in money and time.

  As Mo Siegel of Celestial Seasonings puts it: "Things are going to happen to you that you never expected. You have to count on that and you have to be flexible enough to move around it, or you are going to run into a brick wall and not get past it."

  According to David Liederman, "I deal with the bad news theory of business. I never ask what is right. I only ask what is wrong. Because you have to be able to fix what's wrong before you sit back and open up a bottle of champagne and say, 'I did something right today.' "

  There are two lessons in this observation:

  1. Be detail oriented. Business success is in many respects a result of doing the little things right. The more details you can anticipate doing, the more potential problems you are likely to head off.

2. Keep your cool. If things go wrong early on, remember that you aren't alone in having weird or unfortunate things happen to you.

• *Plan your initial efforts carefully.* The previous chapter emphasized the importance of putting together a written business plan. But beyond having a document that sets out plans and objectives looking ahead three to five years, it is important to know exactly what you want to accomplish during the first few weeks and months you are open for business. That critical time period can make or break your company.

Says James Lowry: "I recommend putting on a piece of paper what are the three to five things that you are going to try to accomplish — today, this week, this quarter, this year — and then work back from those objectives. You start building back in terms of your allocation of your time and allocation of your people's time and in some cases allocation of the client's time to make sure you can accomplish all the things you set out to do in a given time. That is what I really stress with all my people. Set deadlines. Set tough deadlines. Be very realistic about what you can or cannot do within a period of time."

• *Focus on service.* Even if you are not in what is categorized as a service business, you need to focus on providing your customers with a level of service that will make a favorable impression. That means doing what you say you are going to do, when you say you are going to do it.

But in today's supercompetitive world, it often means even more than what you might think would be acceptable. One successful entrepreneur in a service business described his company's challenge this way: "I don't want customers to simply be satisfied with the service we provide. I want them to be ecstatic."

He was taking note of a subtle shift in customers' expectations. They want what you promise — and then some. They want to be pleasantly surprised about your people's attitude, product performance, price, or some other unforeseen benefits. You need to think constantly about ways to pleasantly sur–prise them.

You also need to inquire constantly about what customers like and don't like about what you provide. And you need to obtain the same feedback from prospects who don't buy.

- **Find suppliers you can count on.** You may think because you are paying your suppliers that they will automatically do what you ask and what they promise. Unfortunately, that is not always the case. They may fail to deliver on time. Or they may deliver on time but with a flawed product. Or they may be both late and provide a flawed product.

  Whatever the supplier problem you encounter, it can dam-age your business. My business, for instance, depends heavily on printers to provide the newsletters I put together for clients. My editorial and graphic product can be undone by a printer who delivers the newsletters late, with ink stains, improperly folded, or otherwise not up to my standards. Clients at that point quickly forget the superlative editorial and design work and focus on the printing problems.

  So it is essential that you check out suppliers ahead of time. Ask for references, and call those references. Do some trial runs, if possible, before opening for business. Don't be afraid to tell the supplier what you expect and how important it is that he or she come through for you.

  If your supplier doesn't measure up, don't be afraid to change suppliers. You make that possibility easier if you avoid relying on a single supplier. In my case, for instance, I make it a point to direct at least a small portion of work to a second printer, just in case my primary printer has a fire, goes out of business, or is otherwise unable to provide what I need.

- **Seek long-term relationships with your best suppliers.** Suppliers who provide a top product on time and at a reasonable price quickly become essential to your company's ongoing success. For that reason, it is important to cultivate good suppliers. You do that, first, by paying your bills on time and, second, establishing open lines of communication. The communication part means letting your supplier know as far in advance as possible about an extra or unusually large shipment or if you are going to be late in paying your bill.

  Says Gordon Segal of Crate & Barrel: "I think the most important thing is to realize that you want to build vendor relationships for the long term. So you don't go out in the marketplace and say I will fool him and I will get away with something [by not paying bills]. You never get away with anything, anyplace, anyhow. You really have to build relationships through honesty and working with people on a long-term basis."

- **Establish good credit.** When you seek out suppliers for major orders, they will likely conduct a credit check of your business. If you have been paying your bills on time, they will extend credit to you. If you haven't or simply don't have a credit record because you are just starting out, you may encounter resistance and have to pay for items upon delivery.

  If you don't have a credit record, you may be able to talk your way around the problem, says David Liederman: "If you have no money, you'd better get a piece of publicity pretty fast to let Mr. or Mrs. Supplier know you have a product that has a future so the bills can be paid next week. It is a problem. I am not going to say it isn't a problem. I found that most suppliers, if they believe in you, if they see people buying your products, if they see people writing about your products, will give you a little bit of credit."

  James Lowry recommends a similar tactic in convincing suppliers to do business with you. "When you open your door, people are not going to believe you. They are not going to believe that you are going to do it. I think the best thing — and I think it is why initially I did government work — is I could take the contract, which was a legal document [from] the city of Chicago and later [from] the federal government to the suppliers. I took the actual contract and said, 'We will be paid.' "

Another approach is simply to try to quickly establish credit via prompt payment of your telephone, electricity, rent, and other bills. Then you can refer suppliers to those creditors for references. Or as Christine Martindale of Esprit Miami suggests: "Even if you have enough money to open your own business, you should borrow money from the bank — even if you put it in a money market account, because when you really need it, you are not going to have the credit experience to get it." As discussed in Chapter 7, this will likely involve borrowing against money you already have on deposit.

If all the preceding isn't enough to convince suppliers — and in a tight economy it may not be — then you may be able to compromise by paying for part of your order on delivery and the rest within thirty days. If you strike such a deal, by all means be certain to pay the outstanding amount within the promised thirty days.

- **Watch who you extend credit to.** The other side of the credit coin is your own credit policy. More than one start-up business has been crippled because of its eagerness to fill a large initial order. By failing to do an adequate credit check and/or seek some up-front payment, the company inadvertently became involved with a deadbeat account or a customer that had fallen on hard times and used it as its bank of last resort. For a start-up company that is short of resources at the beginning, failing to get paid for a large order can be disasterous.

- **Re-examine your positioning.** You may think that your entry into the marketplace is happening quietly and unnoticed. But chances are competitors have taken quick and thorough notice of your existence. The managers or owners of competing businesses may pose as customers and telephone you for prices and terms to get a better sense of your position in the marketplace — and your threat to their position.

Within days, your competitors may alter their products or services to match what you have put together. So it is imperative that you be out there in the field watching what is going on — and prepare to improve your service or alter your price as appropriate to keep a step ahead of the marketplace.

■ The Long Term

While this chapter has been devoted to short-term matters concerning when you open for business, there is really a long-term message: You are building the foundation for a long-term source of profits and success. To do that requires establishing relationships — with suppliers, customers, employees, or bankers — built on honesty, integrity, and open communication.

So as you go about trying to conserve cash and making adjustments in your market position, keep in mind that you are setting the stage for an enterprise that will grow and prosper over many years.

■ Exercise: A Strong Start

Answer the following true-or-false questions.

1. During your initial start-up period, it is a good idea
    to bring your suppliers some kind of reassuring
    proof to demonstrate that there is a demand for
    your product or service.   T   F

2. If you don't need credit during your initial start-up,
    do not apply for it.   T   F

3. Don't be very aggressive in going after the first few
    sales. They'll come in time.   T   F

4. Vendors can easily be replaced. Think of them as
    a short-term investment.   T   F

5. Never ask customers or employees what is wrong with
    your business. It only provides them with opportunities
    to complain and take advantage of you.   T   F

6. Goals and objectives should be established on a daily,
    weekly, quarterly, and yearly basis.   T   F

7. It is not necessary to establish and enforce deadlines.
    Somehow the job will get done.   T   F

8. Before you start your business, you should be very
    conscious of possible additional costs and veto as
    many as possible.   T   F

9. Don't get too immersed in details. Chances are,
    everything will go smoothly during your company's
    early days.   T   F

10. One way to keep supply costs down is to switch
    vendors every few months.   T   F

11. During the early stages of growth, the entrepreneur
    should strive to keep his or her business as simple
    as possible.   T   F

12. Being flexible is a sign of weakness. It also shows
    you lack tenacity and strength of character.   T   F

13. Stick with your positioning strategy regardless
    of what your competitors do.   T   F

14. Your supplier wants to see you succeed. If you approach
    him or her and explain that you will be late in paying your
    bill this month, chances are good that he or she will
    extend credit.   T   F

15. Building a strong relationship with customers, suppliers,
    investors, and employees requires honesty and commit-
    ment for the long term.   T   F

Answers:
1. True; 2. False; 3. False; 4. False; 5. False; 6. True; 7. False; 8. True; 9. False; 10. False;
11. True; 12. False; 13. False; 14. True; 15. True.

CHAPTER TEN

LOOKING AHEAD

*"Watching your company will be the
most difficult undertaking of your entire life."*

. . . .

George Gendron, editor-in-chief, *Inc.* Magazine

No matter what stage you're at in preparing to start your own business, you've no doubt heard the warnings:

It's a jungle out there.

Most businesses fail within the first three years.

You've got to be crazy.

It'll be touch and go for a long time.

And on and on.

But, you tell yourself, you'll be different. Your idea is so solid, so original, so well conceived that it can't fail. You'll be like the entrepreneurs featured in this book. You'll overcome the odds and make your business into a huge success.

If this is how you are thinking, then you qualify as what some Harvard Business School professors refer to as an EIH — an entre-preneur-in-heat. No matter how strong the warnings about the challenges you face, you are serene in your confidence. I don't want to diminish your confidence. But I think you should know that whether your business succeeds or fails, it is nearly guaranteed that challenging times lie ahead. Real challenging times. As George

200

Gendron suggests at the beginning of this chapter, watching your own business struggle for survival and growth will be tougher than you ever expected.

To back up his point, Gendron makes an interesting analogy: "Go to an amusement park with a roller coaster. Buy a ticket. Board the ride. Fasten your seat belt and, just before the car starts on that first steep ascent, apply a blindfold. That is what building your business is going to be like emotionally."

I know that I can't give you a complete preview of what to expect as you try to achieve the American dream. No one can. I feel that the only way for someone to appreciate the intensity of feelings involved in starting a business is to experience them personally.

But in this chapter, I do the next best thing. I provide you with a sense of the deep lows and the sharp highs that you can expect through the recollections of some of the entrepreneurs featured in this book. Forewarned is forearmed.

■ The Surprises and Regrets

Even for the successful entrepreneurs featured here, making it was much tougher than any of them expected. Most admit in retrospect that they just didn't realize it was going to be as difficult as it was.

According to George Kachajian of Silicon Technology, "You can't measure the amount of time and effort and thought and anguish and pain that you go through when you start a business." Asked if he was glad he did it, he answers: "I wouldn't trade the experience I have had for anything. But having had the experience, I am not sure I would have done it."

Christine Martindale provides a similarly conflicted answer to whether she would start the same business again: "I don't know if I would do it again. The responsibility is too great. The time re-quired is too great. . . . It requires too much of a commitment. I think now that I have something, I would rather commit my time to something else."

Adding pain to much of the suffering endured by the entrepreneurs along the road to success is that for some, their financial accomplishments came at a significant personal cost. As you read through the recollections of some of our entrepreneurs, appreciate the sense of hurt that permeates their stories.

Most troubling are the family problems that grow out of the start-up process. I pointed out in the previous chapter that starting a business is all-consuming personally, and family members often have trouble dealing with that.

According to Frank Carney, "You pay a personal price for all that excitement and challenge and whatever you get from being an entrepreneur. The sad part of it is you don't know that when you are going in. No one knows that when they are going in."

The result, he adds, is, "You don't have much left for X and X in the rest of your life. That means sleep, that means relaxation, sometimes that means home and family. "

Says James Lowry: "The family suffers because you are not there. You are just not there at the play. And that hurts. And you try to do the best you can and if you have an understanding wife and children, they can be very supportive, but there is a lot of pain when you miss those games and plays."

Perhaps David Liederman sums up the matter best: "You have to be prepared to live on the edge, meaning there is always going to be another crisis, twenty-four hours a day, seven days a week. There are two sides to this story. On the one hand, you are your own boss. On the other hand, the business bosses you and you have to be totally dependent and totally willing, on a moment's notice, to give up whatever you thought you were going to do for a weekend or a night or a morning and jump in and put your finger in the dike and try to keep the business up for another couple of hours before it collapses under its own weight."

■ The Inspiration

Having made my point about the pitfalls of starting a business, I can now share with you our entrepreneurs reflecting on the sense of triumph and glory that comes from establishing a successful growing business. These individuals seem on a personal high much greater than drugs or any other artificial stimulant could provide.

Gordon Segal captures the sense of satisfaction and joy that comes from success: "Being in your own business, you have the wonderful sense of building something and a sense that you can do what you want to do when you want to do it. A sense of having the ability to direct something. . . .You go into your own business as much for the ego gratification of being able to see if your creative juices can create something that people would like and if they applaud you."

Segal contrasts himself with some of his friends who, after nearly thirty years of doing the same thing, "are reaching a midlife crisis. They are bored. I just don't know what to do next, there is so much to accomplish. In a sense, I think that makes it exciting every morning. There is never a time that you are bored in this business, and I think that is one of the great joys of being your own businessperson. . . . I feel like I am twenty-four years old just like I did when I started the business. I think I have the same energy and vigor because my body tells me I better have it to make this thing happen."

Mo Siegel captures the feeling of many successful entrepreneurs when he says, "Owning your own business is... like when you just made a great run down the mountain on your skis, and you cut your path through the powder, and you can do that with a business, the same kind of thing. You feel so good."

■ The Right Stuff

Once you go through the start-up process and hopefully succeed, you will no doubt have your own similes and metaphors to describe the experience. But what does it *really* take to succeed? Certainly it takes many qualities and skills of the sort previously described in this book, not to mention a little bit of luck. But perhaps most important is what might be described as a relentless will to succeed.

Frank Carney describes it this way: "What I look for in an entrepreneur is the — I guess you call it fire in the belly or in the eye. There is a certain fire in the stomach that an entrepreneur has and you can tell it. You know he just can't help but talk about it, and it is coming from within. You know it is not someone who has read it and is talking about it, but it is somebody who is living it and it has consumed him, and you can tell the difference."

Carney even provides a way of determining whether you fit this description: "If you are out selling something and you got 119 nos, would you go to the 120th person? If you are really caught with that burning desire, that number could be 400 and you have got to keep going." (As a truly market-driven entrepreneur, he adds that in such a situation, "I suggest you adjust your package and your pitch to where it fits better.")

Gordon Segal is more succinct in describing the quality: "There is a certain feeling that you want to do it so bad that you are going to overcome whatever you have to overcome."

David Liederman points out that the drive to succeed, whatever you call it or however you describe it, doesn't go away once your business achieves fame and you achieve fortune: "It gets worse. It becomes a drug. You need the aggravation."

He concludes: "What I do for a living is miserable. But it beats working."

■ Exercise: Start-up Word Scramble

Unscramble the following words that describe the start-up experience:

• nacirgattiofi

• sihunag

• tixicnge

• sirsic

• lrelro sarecto

• scentaishuti

• ojy

• inap

Answers: (gratification, anguish, exciting, crisis, roller coaster, enthusiastic, joy, pain)

Index

and incorporation, 107-108, 110-112
and nondisclosure agreement, 66, 172
and offers of stock to employees, 87
and partnerships, 92, 105-107
and patent application, 71
precautions involving, 64-65
and protection of idea, 54-55, 68
and sole proprietorship, 103
and trademark search, 70
Licenses, from state and local
governments, 104
Liederman, David, 15-16, 23-24, 176, 192,
202, 204. *See also* David's Cookies
and credit problems, 195
and delegation of authority, 87
and partnerships, 89
and product, 26, 44
and protection of idea, 61, 63
and research and planning, 32,
34-35, 40, 167
and start-up of business, 24, 191
Life insurance, 106
borrowing against, 146
Loan companies, 159
Loans. *See* Banks; Financing
Lowry, James, 13-14, 189, 202. *See also*
James Lowry Associates
and analysis of competition, 38-39
and appropriate pricing, 134–135, 177
and business plan, 164
and credit problems, 195-196
and initial financing, 145
and marketing, 18-19, 38
and partnerships, 89-91
personal goals of, 13-14
and setting deadlines, 193

M

Magazines, trade, 23
Mail order business, product testing in, 49
Management
concern of venture capitalists for, 155
description of in business plan,
174-175
Manufacturing (of product), and business
plan, 178
Manufacturing business, tasks involved
in, 81
Market niche, and business idea, 18

Market potential, 45-46
discussion of in business plan, 175-176
and venture capitalists, 155
Market research
accessibility of data, 6-7
analysis of competition, 38-40, 49
computerized data bases in, 46, 48
and customer preference, 43-44
data gathering for, 6-7, 45
differing opinions about, 32
government assistance in, 39
keeping notes in, 46
library as resource in, 45
methods and program for, 34-36, 44-50
and opening of business, 42-43
and pricing approaches, 41-42
and product testing, 40-41, 49-50
and prospective customers, 37-38,
46-47, 175
and protection of idea, 55, 58
and size of market, 45-46
tasks involved in, 33
up-to-date information in, 46
and work experience, 35-36
Yellow Pages as reference, 36
Martindale, Christine
and competition, 59
and equity in company, 85
and establishment of credit, 196
experience of in flower business, 35-36
and need for commitment, 187, 188,
201-202
and partnerships, 89, 91-94
and quality of employees, 84
and start-up financing, 149
Mergers, and business plan, 170-171
Mortgages, second, 147

N

Newsletters, labeled as proprietary, 65
New York Times, 35
Noncompete agreement, 61, 66, 67
Nondisclosure agreement, 61, 64
and employees, 66
use of, 65-66
Northern Timber Framing, 145

Other business books from Inc. Magazine

How to *Really* Create A Successful Business Plan
by David E. Gumpert

Anatomy of A Start-Up:
27 Real-Life Case Studies:
Why Some New Businesses Succeed
And Others Fail
Edited by Elizabeth K. Longsworth

301 Great Management Ideas
From America's Most Innovative
Small Companies
Introduction by Tom Peters
Edited by Sara P. Noble

To receive a complete listing of Inc. Business
Books and Videos, please call **1-800-372-0018
ext. 4118.** Or write to **Inc. Business Products,**
P.O. Box 1365, Wilkes-Barre, PA 18703-1365.